Wigmore Hall · 1901-2001 · A Celebration

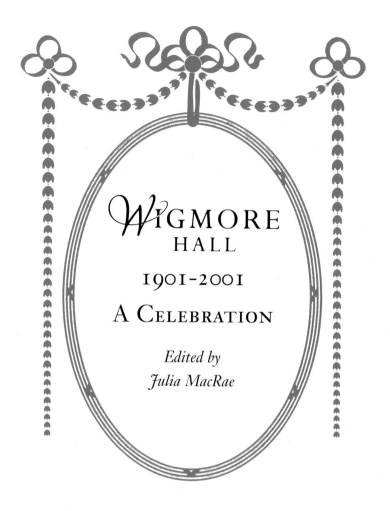

WIGMORE HALL

1901-2001

A CELEBRATION

*Edited by
Julia MacRae*

THE WIGMORE HALL TRUST

LONDON

Contents

JULIA MacRae

Preface and Acknowledgements

Planning and editing this book has been pure pleasure because everyone with whom I have been in contact has had in common a love for the Wigmore Hall and a desire to be involved with its centenary. From the start the book was conceived not as the definitive history but as a celebration, in which as many aspects of the Hall as possible could be brought together and shared. The Hall's famously passionate devotees will argue forever about what should or should not have been included, just as they argue about the merits of this or that performance – that is one of the civilised delights of the place. I hope that many of the memories the book evokes will provoke further spirited comment. I hope, too, that some duplication of material will be understood and excused – it was inevitable that certain themes would recur, most noticeably the acoustic, the audience, and the excellence of William Lyne! Impossible to 'edit' out these elements as they are bound to be commented on again and again, especially by the artists and the Friends.

There may be some who wonder at the use of Arthur, and not Artur, for Rubinstein, but according to his biographer, Harvey Sachs, 'Arthur' was Rubinstein's own preference.

I am most grateful to all the contributors, artists, and Friends who, in spite of their own busy schedules, managed to be exemplary in keeping to deadlines with their copy. The time and trouble they have all taken is very much appreciated. If I single out Professor Cyril Ehrlich for thanks it is because he cheerfully completed his chapter on the Hall's history regardless of surgery during the period of writing. Thanks are also due to John Tusa and the Trustees for their support and encouragement, and of course to William Lyne and the staff of Wigmore Hall, in particular Derek Archer, Paula Best and Andy Payne. My personal thanks for 'creative listening' to Dame Janet Baker, Alan Lee, Gabrielle Macphedran, Adam Hopkins, Delia Huddy and Siam Chowkwanyun.

To the designer Douglas Martin I owe my especial thanks. He and I have worked together on many projects, none more rewarding than this. As always, I am indebted to him for his expertise – and also on this occasion for his fluent German! Ilsa Yardley's generous and professional help with proof-reading has been invaluable. Toby Colbourne of the excellent printers BAS in Hampshire has been consistently helpful.

Leaving the Hall after a concert one night I overheard the following comment: 'If Heaven is not like the Wigmore Hall I'm not going there.' What better note on which to begin this book.

Wigmore Hall –
A Celebration

Dame Janet Baker

Foreword

Anyone who has ever sung in the bath or has had to speak in front of others knows the sheer exhilaration of a good acoustic and a supportive audience.

You would be surprised how rare these things are and places where they can be found together even more so. Musicians, swapping experiences, usually have their list of favourites, never a very long one, but a name which crops up regularly on most of them is the Wigmore Hall.

I wish we knew what illusive balance between plaster and wood and what proportion of floor to ceiling actually creates a marvellous acoustic. Mathematically accurate measurements and good design take us only so far, after which it's a question of luck. Like a fingerprint, the great venues of the world are individually unique and performances are remembered as special and cherished occasions. Mostly, one struggles. The musician knows the moment he places a finger on the keyboard, draws bow over the string or opens his mouth to sing whether he will be inspired to his best work or reduced to something rather less. If the former, it is likely to be better than his best; if the latter, a battle to the death.

Naturally any musician wants to return again and again to those buildings where he feels upheld, nurtured and encouraged, this is why so many demonstrate such enduring loyalty to the Wigmore Hall. When artists find the right circumstances enabling them to give of their best, the depth of communication which results eventually permeates the very bricks and mortar; in time an atmosphere is created, a tangible thing, affecting everything that happens there. You feel it at the Wigmore Hall just walking through the door onto the curious, apse-shaped platform, even before a single note is played.

To be on good form in a great hall is wonderful, but still only half the equation. The words 'You've got a full house tonight' are always magic to the ear; when the audience is also a discerning one the scene is set for a shared experience to be treasured in the heart, mind and memory. The Wigmore audience hears most of the famous musicians of world class; it also hears many relatively unknown ones. I don't know which is the more moving experience – to see the obvious devotion shown when an established old friend steps out onto the platform, or to feel the sympathetic support offered to a young untried performer.

The Wigmore audience, willing to tread the less well-known paths of unfamiliar repertoire, provides a golden opportunity; programme building for this audience is especially rewarding precisely because the artist feels it is possible to experiment, widening the boundaries, developing understanding. There is no greater compliment than this; both artist and audience can explore fresh fields together and attempt to find a right balance between familiar repertoire and the new. It is not easy to achieve and demands commitment, but the unwavering loyalty of those who, season after season, support the concerts at the Wigmore Hall, is legendary and it is based on trust – the trust they feel in one person, William Lyne.

They know that his commitment is also unwavering; so is his absolute concern for quality; and they know he has never let them down. He is the person who has created the climate for all that happens in this building; it has earned him an unrivalled reputation together with the respect, admiration and love from his artists and his audience. He has a sort of genius, which, like the elusive beauty of his hall's acoustic, is hard to analyse or explain. We are infinitely grateful to him, his staff and to all the Friends.

The pursuit of excellence is alive and kicking in Wigmore Street, a marvellous start for the next one hundred years.

William Lyne

WILLIAM LYNE

Looking Back – A Personal View

Wigmore Hall exerts magic. A magic which extends over its audiences and its musicians. It exerted its magic over 12,000 miles to me in Australia, where I was fascinated by advertisements for Wigmore Hall concerts in my subscription copies of the *Sunday Times* and the *Observer*. Arriving in London in 1957, on a year's leave of absence from my post with the Australian Broadcasting Commission in Sydney, I made straight for the Hall on the first morning and booked tickets for Gérard Souzay partnered by Dalton Baldwin, and pianists Shura Cherkassky and Robert Goldsand. The memory of that first concert is still with me; the Hall's unique atmosphere, the size, very different from the Victorian Sydney Town Hall; and, what is more, the house lights did not go down, which seemed very strange. Years later, I came to realise from comments made by visiting musicians that Europe is not plentifully supplied with intimate halls blessed with the Wigmore's acoustics and rapport with its audiences.

A few months later I heard from a friend, Terry Palmer (later to be orchestra manager of the London Symphony Orchestra and subsequently manager of Henry Wood Hall), with whom I had travelled to England and who was working at Ibbs and Tillett the concert agents, that Wigmore Hall was looking for an Assistant Manager. I applied and was interviewed by the manager, H.T.C. Brickell and the Arts Council's music director, John Denison. 'He's the one I want,' was Mr Brickell's verdict. This very quiet, very young, Australian, who hardly opened his mouth! Fate!

So what was the Hall like in those initial days as Assistant Manager? My introduction to Lieder had been through the recordings of Lotte Lehmann and Elisabeth Schumann. Lotte Lehmann was still alive but had long stopped singing. Nevertheless, I had always hoped that she would return to Australia, which she had toured in the past, maybe for master classes; then I would at least see and hear her. The very first per-

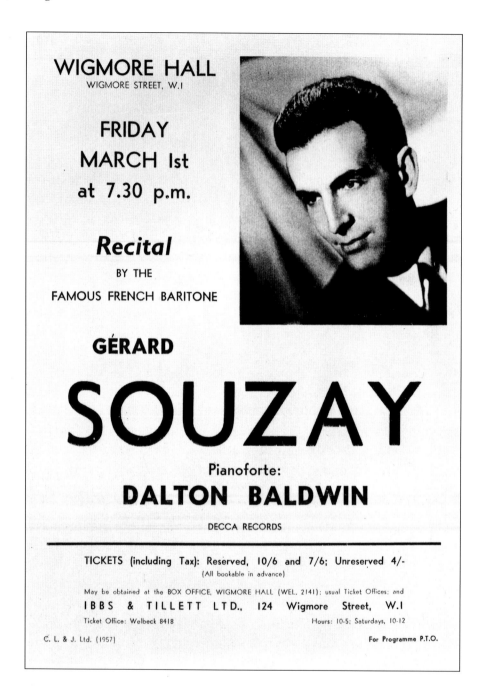

William Lyne's introduction to Wigmore Hall, 1957

formances I managed in my new post at the Wigmore were Lotte Lehmann master classes! At these classes, there were twelve in all, Lotte Lehmann intoned the songs and arias she was teaching; tenor, soprano, bass, mezzo, it did not matter, in fact I suspected that she relished the opportunity to perform arias such as Don José's 'Flower Song' from *Carmen*. At one lesson on her most famous role, the Marschallin in *Der Rosenkavalier*, she broke into full voice and the whole audience burst into applause. Lotte Lehmann returned two years later; this second set of classes introduced both Janet Baker and Grace Bumbry, the latter gave a recital when the classes had finished. I know that Dame Janet was not very happy about the classes but I recall that she contributed a memorable and moving performance of Schumann's *Frauenliebe und -leben*.

Mr Brickell had joined the Hall in 1918 and had been Manager since 1932. There was also a wonderful man called Mr Lake who had looked after the artists backstage and turned the music pages since 1903. He had a fund of stories about artists and would always have a post-concert whisky with Gerald Moore after one of Gerald's appearances. At the Hall's 50th anniversary celebrations, Gerald made sure that Mr Lake was on

Gerald Moore

stage and brought him forward for his own bow to the audience. It was very reassuring for Elly Ameling to be told by Mr Lake at her first London recital that she reminded him of Elisabeth Schumann (Elly still remembers it) or for a worried pianist to be told that Busoni had made the same mistake.

At that time, artists were never engaged, the Hall was hired for all concerts and there could be five piano recitals in one week. The Hall had acquired a reputation for debut recitals but buried among the new artists there were in fact some splendid concerts. The annual concert by Julian Bream and George Malcolm had become an institution. Mieczyslaw Horszowski, who has returned in more recent years for several memorable concerts when in his nineties, gave a series of Mozart piano sonata recitals. There were recitals by Julian Bream and John Williams. I had only been there two months before Christa Ludwig made her debut with Gerald Moore and the debuts of Janet Baker and Jacqueline du Pré were to follow during the next few years. Both Alfred Brendel and the Hungarian Quartet gave Beethoven cycles. I rushed home after a Saturday matinée full of enthusiasm for a wonderful new ensemble, the Beaux Arts Trio.

Shura Cherkassky appeared regularly in the London Pianoforte Series. Two other pianists whom I remember with particular affection were Lili Kraus, outstanding in Mozart and Schubert, and Kathleen Long: very English, no fuss, no frills, just wonderful music making. There were also pianists who had been giving annual Wigmore recitals for many years. Gertrude Peppercorn for instance, whose first concerts were back in the Bechstein Hall days, before the First World War, but Frank Merrick held the record. His first Wigmore recital had been in 1903, two years after the Hall opened. All artists expected at least two press notices, very different to the situation today when exceptional new musicians can make their debuts and pass without being noticed by the press. This is because of the attitude of many of the arts editors, not of individual critics who deplore this situation. There is now a huge public for music. Do editors feel that concert-goers do not want to read about the concerts they attend? I feel that they do.

It was so frustrating that by now potential audiences identified the Hall with debut recitals and did not realise that these other concerts were

Beaux Arts Trio

happening. Music lovers would read reviews in the national press, telephone to ask about obtaining a concert diary, and would be told that there was no such publication.

In 1966 when the kindly Harry Brickell retired I was asked by the Arts Council what my plans for the Hall would be if the Arts Council were to appoint me Manager. The changes I had been anxious to implement were outlined and that was that! The job was mine. Needless to say, one of my first changes was to print a monthly concert diary. Wigmore Hall advertisements were scattered all over the concert pages. After much persuasion, the formidable Emmie Tillett agreed to insert her concerts under one main Wigmore Hall heading. At that time her concert agency, Ibbs and Tillett, had so many concerts at the Hall that many people thought she owned it. Ticket sales were centralised through the Hall and Sunday evening concerts were introduced with a concert by the New Vienna String Quartet. And of course I thought that these and other changes would have an instant effect and audiences would improve, but it took several years. The auditorium was entirely painted in what I referred to as bathroom green; with the advice of an architect, the colours were changed in the auditorium, foyer and on the street canopy. The gas lights made the auditorium resemble a hospital ward. They were altered to the gas fittings that can still be seen in the Hall today.

I had taken over as Manager of Wigmore Hall on 24 October 1966. The next few years were very difficult. There was no money for artists' fees so somehow I had to persuade musicians I admired to give concerts. Many artists wanted to appear at the Hall but did not want to be surrounded by debut recitals. When my first full season opened in 1967, Peter Pears and Benjamin Britten gave the opening concert. I well remember the white and gold programme cover we produced and the lady from Bristol who wrote to complain of the outrageous cost, two shillings. How I managed to get permission to promote this concert I cannot imagine. In October 1967 we also had a wonderful Sunday evening performance to celebrate the 25th anniversary of the Apollo Society. The evening was called *Cardinal Virtues, Deadly Sins*, devised by George Rylands and with an unrepeatable cast of actors and musicians: Peggy Ashcroft, Jill Balcon, Edith Evans, Irene Worth, John Gielgud, Marius Goring, C. Day Lewis, Patrick Wymark (replacing Michael Redgrave), Natasha Litvin, piano, and Robert Spencer, lute. Very expensive tickets, top price 30 shillings. Poetry and music recitals occurred at regular intervals with notable actors and musicians. For these programmes to be successful it is essential that they should be devised by someone who understands the format, such as George Rylands or John Carroll, who were both splendid.

In March 1967, five months after my appointment as Manager, the Queen Elizabeth Hall had opened and there was a feeling that the Wigmore would suffer. Indeed many artists did take their concerts and series there. But many musicians stood by me. The Lindsay Quartet, Julian Bream, John Williams, John Ogdon and several others. Raymond Lewenthal, an American pianist, made quite a stir when he gave a number of Liszt and Alkan recitals. The Hall was sold out for all of his concerts, for which he appeared in a black cloak and with hardly any light on stage. The *Observer* music critic wrote, 'There was a queue for tickets down Wigmore Street before the Queen Elizabeth Hall sounds the death knell of Wigmore Hall.'

Peter Pears and Benjamin Britten

I was furious – 'I'll see if it does' – but in the event the new hall was beneficial; audiences, used only to attending orchestral concerts, started exploring recitals and chamber music performances. Competition is good, in my case it goaded me to strive even harder.

There was a dearth of chamber music in London in those days and this was something I really wanted to address. The Hall had far too many piano recitals. Song recitals were the least popular events although the occasional appearance by a well-known singer would draw a good, but not capacity, audience. So concerts gradually improved. Alfred Brendel returned and we had recitals by Janet Baker, Alfreda Hodgson, Julian Bream, John Williams, Moura Lympany, Richard Goode, Robert Tear and Nelson Freire. György Pauk, Ralph Kirshbaum and Peter Frankl emerged in the seventies. Julius Katchen played the complete piano works of Brahms and also presented, in 1971, his protégé Pascal Rogé, aged 19, in his first London appearance. Gerald Moore appeared regularly and gave his lecture recital *Am I Too Loud?*. His timing in the lecture recitals was wonderful, he could have been an actor. One of our artists' rooms is named after Gerald. David Munrow's Early Music Consort appeared as the early music movement evolved. Mitsuko Uchida performed the complete Mozart piano sonatas and her career was launched. Peter Pears and Benjamin Britten, ever loyal, returned for more recitals. When a rumour circulated that the Hall was under threat of demolition, Britten asked if there was anything he could do to help.

I devised a system whereby artists could appear at the Hall without having to hire it and set about persuading artists and their managers to take part.

Mitsuko Uchida

There would be no set fee but they would definitely receive some pay-ment, this was guaranteed. They would not end up with a large bill after the concert, but to do this I had to be able to gauge the box office draw-ing power of both the artists and the programmes so that neither the artists nor the Hall would lose money. A series of concerts 'to introduce the season' was arranged. They were successful and John Cruft, the Music Director of the Arts Council, encouraged me to arrange more. Over the ensuing years the programming gradually developed, although there were severe restrictions on any variation of the advertising and publicity.

The number of chamber music concerts started to increase as we worked with ensembles such as the Gabrieli, Melos and Fitzwilliam Quar-tets. The Fitzwilliam were invited to play the complete Shostakovich Quartets, a cycle which was very successful and well attended. Eventually I convinced the Arts Council (which had acquired a lease on the Hall in 1946 when, I believe, the BBC was about to take it over to use as a studio) that I should at least be able to offer a fee for the opening concert of the season, but this was not until 1975. Opening concerts included the Melos Ensemble, the Beaux Arts Trio, Alicia de Larrocha, and then we estab-lished the tradition of opening each season with a singer, Elly Ameling, Brigitte Fassbaender, Margaret Price, Jessye Norman (twice) amongst others.

For many years we were a staff of four: the Manager, Assistant Manager, Box Office Manager and Box Office Assistant. I did all of the accounts, balanced the books, dealt with wages and in-come tax, in addition to booking the concerts. Assistant Managers have included Jeremy Tyndall, now Festivals' Administrator at Cheltenham and Paul Davies, presently General Manager of St John's, Smith Square.

Jessye Norman

András Schiff

In 1975, András Schiff won third prize in the Leeds International Piano Competition. In an interview after the Competition he said, 'I knew I would not win because I played Bach on the piano, but I do not care, I only care about my Bach.' I thought, That's the man for me, contacted his manager next morning, booked András for a performance of the *Goldberg Variations* and we went on from there. András Schiff's music making has wound like a thread through our concert seasons in the ensuing years. He stands for everything I like to think Wigmore Hall is about. No circus tricks, just making music and communicating with our audiences. He carries on the tradition of the great musicians who appeared here in the past, the Busch Quartet, Artur Schnabel, Edwin Fischer. He is a great artist, a genius, equally inspiring in recitals, concerts and chamber music; one of the few soloists who can successfully partner singers. His duo with Peter Schreier is one of the outstanding partnerships of our time. But, most important of all, the music always comes first. Through the last 25 years he has brought several festivals to the Wigmore, major Bach series, the complete Schubert sonatas twice. He has enriched us with Haydn and Bartók and increased our admiration of their qualities. András devised both our Schubert Bi-Centenary Concert in 1979 and the Hall's own Centenary Concert in 2001.

Seven concerts were arranged to celebrate Wigmore Hall's 75th Anniversary celebrations in 1976 and they proved to be a turning point. 'Do you think Arthur Rubinstein would give our 75th Anniversary Concert?' 'Write to Paris and ask him,' replied Wilfrid Van Wyck, Rubinstein's manager. Rubinstein accepted and refused to take either a fee or expenses: 'I want to help the Hall.' His first London recitals had been at the Wigmore in May 1912 and he went on to give many more in subsequent years. The distinguished soprano Emmy Destinn was in the audience in May 1912, as was the violinist Jacques Thibaud. Rubinstein's recital of Beethoven, Schumann, Ravel and Chopin on 31 May 1976 was his last concert appearance. At the end of his recital he announced his retirement, thanked the audience for their support over the years, and entreated them to 'keep coming back to this wonderful hall'. He was one of the most charming people I have ever met.

We have much to thank Rubinstein for. The success of the concerts with artists like Rubinstein, Peter Pears, Murray Perahia, Julian Bream, Elisabeth Schwarzkopf and Henryk Szeryng encouraged more and more artists to appear at the Wigmore. The excitement of that 75th Anniversary Concert on 31 May, with NBC television in attendance, at last showed the Arts Council just what could be done with the Hall.

In 1977, Hannah Horovitz, who at that time was an artists' manager, proposed a short series of Sunday Morning Coffee Concerts. We went so far as to announce them in the concert diary, but the funding did not materialise. In 1978 a Summer Festival was arranged with the co-operation of the Arts Council and Eleanor Warren was appointed as Artistic Director. This was a huge success, many of the concerts were sold out. It was then that the Sunday Morning Coffee Concerts were revived. At first, Coffee Concerts were programmed every summer but they were so popular that I decided to programme them throughout the year.

The 1979/80 season saw the appearance of our first subscription series with a theme: Gabriel Fauré. I dearly wanted to arrange this but knew that if I mentioned it to a committee there would always be someone who would object so I just went ahead. The complete chamber music of Fauré was presented together with a selection of the songs and the piano music. The series was a huge success, 22 concerts; this exploration was something that really needed to be done. The descriptions and verdicts in books, on the neglected chamber music in particular, proved to be very unreliable. In performance these works were often quite striking, although many of them do rely on the sensitivity and empathy of the performers. I wanted the almost forgotten chamber music version of the song cycle *La bonne chanson* to be performed as well as that with piano accompaniment. Amelia Freedman, artistic director of The Nash Ensemble, has always been willing to collaborate and to discuss projects. The Nash and Sarah Walker agreed to perform the chamber version and subsequently went on to record *La bonne chanson* very successfully. There is no doubt that Fauré's music has been performed much more frequently since this series, at least at the Wigmore.

Throughout all of this period we were sustained by an Arts Council grant. Without that Arts Council grant it would have been difficult to progress and to achieve whatever success we may have had in the following years. The grant paid for the wages and some of the basic expenses. For this I have always been grateful.

From these beginnings the regular Wigmore series developed: the Song, Chamber Music, Early Music & Baroque and the London Pianoforte Series. We explored British music, French, American, Scandinavian Song, Purcell, Bartók, Mozart, Haydn, Schumann, Dvořák was paired with Grieg, the complete Britten Songs and many more. The Nash Ensemble went on to give a series of concerts every season, each with a theme and sometimes complementing our own themes. Elly Ameling gave two recitals every autumn. Elly always put the music first; she was incredibly versatile. One expected her to sing Lieder and French song, but she was equally impressive in Spanish and North American music. Her performance of Satie's *La Diva de l'Empire* is the funniest I have ever heard and seen, especially when she gently lifted her skirt – so unexpected from Elly. We presented our first Song Recital Series which was successful but as it progressed I thought this is all very well but what about the next Series? Somehow it fell into place, and so it went on season after season, with my inviting various singers. The Songmakers' Almanac appeared regularly and Graham Johnson encouraged our patrons to extend their knowledge of the repertoire. Brigitte Fassbaender had never given a recital in this country. She came and gave her first London recital and has stayed with us ever since. Margaret Price seemed to spend most of her time singing in other countries. Margaret gave the first of many wonderful recitals at the Hall. Régine Crespin had a huge success. Eventually many of the concert managers approached me. I still invite great singers who rarely appear in this country but nowadays much time is spent looking for outstanding new musicians as well.

I have learnt that if one really believes in an artist or ensemble then it is important to pursue that belief and take no notice of any adverse criticisms. In the end everyone will come around and the press will have forgotten its initial reactions. The obverse is true as well; do not rely on enthusiastic reviews, especially of recordings. The reality can be very different. In addition there are some artists who do not take to the recording studio; they either need an audience or the microphone cannot capture their personalities. The best way to judge an artist is to listen to the music itself.

In 1979 the Takács Quartet won the Portsmouth (now the London) International String Quartet Competition and gave a Wigmore concert a few days afterwards. We fell in love with them immediately and the Quartet has gone on to become part of the Wigmore family. They are not resident in name, it is not necessary because they are in spirit.

And so we went on. Colleagues in the concert world would tell me that 'the Wigmore is doing well' but I would never believe them. I was not satisfied and would always think of ways in which we could be doing better. It is only in more recent years that I have felt able to admit that, yes, we are successful.

In April 1993 we became an independent trust and a registered charity. Our first Chairman, Sir Trevor Holdsworth, formed our board, steered us through the charity registration and safely over all the hurdles and risks of becoming independent. We successfully weathered the financial hurdles as well. Working as an independent trust has given me more freedom. We have an ideal Chairman, John Tusa, and board members who are supportive and always ready to help with major problems. There are the wonderful contributions of the Friends of Wigmore Hall, the

Rubinstein Circle, the Advisory Council and a number of enlightened sponsors. Individuals such as Jackie Rosenfeld, a Trustee who works tirelessly on our behalf, Valerie Barber, our enthusiastic publicist, and Julia MacRae, who both suggested and edited this book. Julia is a Trustee and is also Co-ordinator of the Friends Volunteers. Dr Ralph Kohn whose Foundation has made the Wigmore International Song Competition possible. And our superb, dedicated musicians with whom it is a pleasure to work.

Rather than produce a catalogue of the great musicians, series and festivals we have presented in subsequent years, I should like to recall some of the special moments that have lingered in my mind for years afterwards. Our audiences must also have their own special memories.

Mieczyslaw Horszowski in his late nineties showing us how Schumann should be played and giving concerts that distilled the essence of a lifetime's music making. The Haydn Festivals: András Schiff's Festival when we had trios, solos, songs, a cantata etc. and on each evening a late Haydn string quartet to look forward to at the end of the concert, played by the Takács Quartet. The Lindsays' Haydn Festival when Peter Cropper enthused about the music before each performance. These Festivals changed the way we viewed Haydn so that when the complete Haydn string quartets from op. 20 onwards were programmed many of the concerts were sold out. Shura Cherkassky, the spontaneity of his concerts, he needed an audience to give of his best. Just before he went on stage for the last Wigmore concert of his I attended he looked nervous; and said, 'Every concert is like my debut', wonderful to be so fresh after a long career. Alfred Brendel showing in a set of Variations that Beethoven could be funny. Milan Škampa of the

Shura Cherkassky with William Lyne

Smetana Quartet launching into Dvořák's *American* Quartet on the composer's own viola. This repertoire was in the Quartet's blood, they played without music. Steven Isserlis playing the Cello Sonata of Rachmaninov. Geoffrey Parsons sending shivers up and down my spine as he played the accompaniment to Schubert's *Die Stadt* (*Schwanengesang*). The complete Schubert Piano Sonatas and String Quartets. Schubert has figured prominently in our programmes over the last 34 years. It could be that this reflects the tastes of the

Christa Ludwig

Director. I never cease to wonder at Schubert's genius. One commentator in the *Guardian* went so far as to say that perhaps the Hall should be called St Franz of Wigmore Street.

And a host of memories from vocal concerts. A sudden individual turn of phrase from Peter Schreier in Schubert's *Der Musensohn*. For me, Schreier is one of the great Lieder singers of our day. The music is all there, nothing is overdone. The long silence after Brigitte Fassbaender's performance of *Winterreise*. Christa Ludwig's thrilling performance of Richard Strauss's *Zueignung* (when she sang it again as an encore a few seasons later I commented that no one had performed it as well since. The reply came quickly: 'I'm very glad to hear it!'). A very moving Strauss evening with Felicity Lott. Time standing still in the Hall when Ann Murray sang Schumann's *Mondnacht* during one of Graham Johnson's Summer Song Cycles. Introducing Matthias Goerne; the audience reminding me as they arrived: 'He had better be good, you recommended him;' sitting in my seat worrying, as usual, whether people would like the concert; but then we had his incomparable performance of Schubert's *Totengräbers Heimweh*. Standing at the back of the auditorium for a Kathleen Ferrier Competition and hearing a very young Ian Bostridge for the first time. A ravishing young soprano singing Schubert's *Der Hirt auf dem*

Felsen at a Trinity College graduation ceremony. Her name? Margaret Price. Anne Sofie von Otter's chilling performance of *Erlkönig* and her riotous *Cabaret Songs* by Benjamin Britten. Jessye Norman singing a spiritual when, as a friend of mine remarked, 'You could feel the electricity running down underneath the Hall and up through every seat.' Peter Pears at his final Wigmore Hall recital, with Murray Perahia, transforming Haydn's *English Canzonettas*. Elisabeth Schwarzkopf, with superb support from Geoffrey Parsons, opening her recital in our 75th Anniversary celebrations with Hugo Wolf's *Kennst du das Land*; I knew at the time that I would never hear such a shattering interpretation of this song again. During an interview in a BBC programme shortly after the Hall's anniversary, she was asked what had struck her most about returning to the Hall. She replied, 'The Hall's fabulous acoustics of course. The acoustics were so wonderful that I think that people hadn't heard me at the Festival Hall, they heard me here for the first time.' It was true, the recital was a completely different experience to those I had previously heard.

This is what live music making is all about. These experiences happen in a hall where you can actually hear the music and the audience can almost take part in the performance. When I commented on a particularly striking part of his performance to Peter Wiley, at that time cellist of the Beaux Arts Trio, he replied that 'the Wigmore dares you to excel yourself.' Quartets say how wonderful it is to play in; singers to sing in. Many artists have said that the Hall is their musical home.

Thomas Collcutt, the architect of Wigmore Hall, certainly knew what he was doing. Stand on the stage and one can just feel the communication with an audience. There is the same effect on the stage of the Palace Theatre, also designed by Collcutt, and at the Musikverein in Vienna.

My work as Director has been very gratifying. I can look around me and see the rapt faces of the audience at concerts. The success of a great artist or of a new musician whom I have introduced can be very moving. There is that wonderful Wigmore welcome as the artists walk on stage. These are all experiences of which I never tire. The patrons who wrote to me when we were closed for sixteen months for additions to the building; those who still write with words of appreciation, are important. They show that the work we do at the Wigmore does make a difference, their response encourages us to do more. Many of the staff are dedicated

'*A Wigmore Lyne-up*': Ian Bostridge, Felicity Lott, Graham Johnson, William Lyne, Matthias Goerne

Cecilia Bartoli with William Lyne

and committed to the success of the Hall, they stay with me for a long time. Peter Williamson, our designer and print buyer, has worked with us for twenty years. Some visiting musicians say that we are like a family; that is because the staff take an interest in everything we do and work for the success of the Hall. We have a family of musicians too, I do not need to tell the regulars who they are. They come because they want to make music and not for some fabulous fee. Some artists never change, they are just as nice now as when they first appeared.

As I said earlier, this chapter in our centenary book is not a history of the series, festivals and individual concerts I have arranged during my thirty-four years as Wigmore Hall director but rather a personal retrospect of the early days and of how the present concert seasons developed. In 1976 there were seven 75th Anniversary Concerts. For the centenary in 2001 there are fifty-four. I hope that in this chapter I may have also provided a glimpse of the magic I referred to in the first sentence and how it affects our musicians, audiences and staff. That is so far as any of this can be put into words; for many of us our feelings about music are very personal.

On the occasion of the centenary I should like to say thank you to everyone who has supported Wigmore Hall: musicians, audience, the Trust, staff, the Friends, sponsors, trusts, foundations, concert managers, designer, publicist, the BBC with whom we have a close relationship, the Arts Council, London Arts and The City of Westminster.

Cyril Ehrlich

The First Hundred Years

A great concert hall acquires its own distinctive image, earned over the years by providing an agreeable home for good music and discriminating audiences. An appropriate history must be something more than a parade of stars, for distinguished artists have performed in many a place which commands no such distinction or loyalty. Better read it as a mirror of past music making and listening, though that too is insufficient, for mirrors merely reflect, while a great hall creates and changes concert life. Over the centuries London's music has acquired and lost a diversity of venues, but for serious musicians and music lovers Wigmore Hall is unique: no surviving place can remotely match it in their affection and respect.

§ *Bechstein Hall: redefining concert life.* Bechstein Hall, designed by Thomas Collcutt, one of the finest architects of his day, was opened in 1901 with a name which immediately furnished ample and appropriate associations of quality, for Bechstein was Europe's leading piano maker, its instruments preferred by most pianists outside America, where Steinway predominated. And this was a matter of profound resonance at a time when music flourished and pianos were not only widely purchased but universally acknowledged as central to cultural and social life, on and off the concert platform. A generation later Noël Coward's hymn to 'The Stately Homes of England' would insist, with typical precision, that the pawnable family grand was inevitably a Bechstein. Meanwhile the house of Bechstein was simply attaching a concert space to its showrooms and suite of studios, already thronging with customers who would soon be purchasing half of its considerable output. In similar fashion a Berlin predecessor had been inaugurated a few years earlier by von Bülow, renowned pianist and conductor, intimate friend of Carl Bechstein and closely associated with the design of his instruments. Brahms was in the audience and returned to give the second recital with Joachim. The London Hall could not quite match that inauguration, but it did offer two prestigious opening concerts, with adjustments to local tastes. On Friday 31 May 1901, Helen Trust, esteemed singer of drawing-room ballads, opened with the National Anthem, and returned with three representative samples of her fashionable genre. The rest of the programme was more demanding. Busoni, doyen of artist-scholar-composer-pianists, began a lifelong association with the Hall in Beethoven's Sonata op. 109. Then the tenor Raymund von Zur-Mühlen, who had studied with Clara Schumann and was soon to settle in England, sang three Schubert songs, including *Erlkönig*. Busoni returned to play Bach's F minor Violin Sonata with the venerated Ysaÿe. Unaccompanied Bach and the Beethoven Romance in G (with piano accompaniment in the manner of the day) completed the violinist's contribution, and Busoni finished with the Brahms Paganini Variations. Accompanists suitable to such an occasion were Victor Beigel and Hamilton Harty. Saturday afternoon's celebration was 'lighter', with three platform idols and Landon Ronald as accompanist. Ben Davies delivered the National Anthem, Beethoven's *Adelaide*, and a Schumann group. Plunket Greene offered songs by Parry and Stanford. Pachmann, already renowned for 'touch' and tone, but not yet for clowning, played Weber's Sonata op. 39 and some short pieces by Schumann and Chopin.

The Hall was promoted with proud assurance as the best of places for intimate music making, seating 580 in conditions of unprecedented comfort and safety 'for both the audience and the performer'. It challenged London's tradition of 'stern and stereotyped discomfort . . . draughty halls and uncomfortable seats . . . faulty acoustics.' Its visual delights – most particularly the platform's cupola, designed by Gerald Moira, with its 'Genius of Harmony' ball of fire – were heaped with adjectives. The heating and ventilation system bespoke modernity, 'identical with that favoured by the great London hospitals', allowing audiences to 'listen to the divinest harmonies in a state of perfect immunity of all unhygienic elements.' In sum it was 'the most commodious and, from an acoustic standpoint, the most perfect concert-hall in London.' The publicist's words were immediately endorsed in a chorus of welcome throughout the press. Since practically every newspaper and journal then devoted ample space to music, brimming with opinionated critical comment (but no interviews), an abundance of words was bestowed upon the city's 'handsomest concert room'; the 'most sumptuously comfortable place of its kind to be found'. Particular approval greeted the placing of 'the artists' rooms on the same level so that singers will not have to arrive breathless on the platform.' Even the *Athenaeum*, reactionary and always hard to please, agreed that it 'sounds well' and that if at times there was too much reverberation, then that was surely because artists had not yet made themselves at home. They rapidly proceeded to do so as the good news spread throughout the world of music.

Timing and location for this initiative were well chosen. Concert life in London was beginning to enjoy a belated process of innovation, necessarily part of a thoroughgoing revolution in leisure and entertainment, based in the 'West End', and particularly near Oxford Circus. Public transport was efficient, cheap, and at hand. There were lavishly innovative theatres and music halls, soon to include the Coliseum and Palladium. A wide public was being introduced to the experience of shopping for pleasure in new-style department stores, before long to be dwarfed by the enormous, multi-purpose Selfridges. Even informal eating places, seldom good in London, particularly for unchaperoned women, were being transformed, notably by Lyons tea shops and 'corner houses', their supply centre incidentally occupying a disused piano factory. Nearby in Langham Place, the recently opened Queen's Hall, built for music, was attracting musicians and audiences, including many newcomers, with a transformed environment: unprecedented standards of comfort, continuous concert promotion and dedicated management. Until then concert-goers had been forced to subsist on the traditional short season, a few months of sporadic events in spartan conditions – a meagre diet of 'Pops' at the noisy, sometimes noisome, St James Hall, Piccadilly, supplemented for the hardiest enthusiasts by train journeys to the discomfort of temporary concert spaces in a vast arena at the Crystal Palace, Sydenham. Lifetimes of such listening were subsequently romanticised in many a reminiscence, but by later standards they lacked consistency and sustenance. Now an abundance of professionally organised music making was suddenly on offer at a sensible location. Robert Newman and Henry Wood, Nikisch and the London Symphony Orchestra, and new-style international concert agents were filling the annual calendar with symphony concerts and celebrity recitals including, of course, a ground-breaking long summer of Proms. The weekly diary was also transformed, with Saturdays busier than ever and, most remarkably, Sunday concerts, since Sabbatarianism had at last suffered defeat.

This sudden efflorescence of symphony concerts and the proliferation of orchestras unique to London were the most spectacular newcomers. But an endless stream of smaller groups and soloists were also eager to perform, and subsequently boast of performing – a most significant influence on supply – in the great metropolis. If Queen's Hall could house those with sufficient drawing power, or aspiration, to market some 2,500 seats, there was obvious scope for a comparable, but smaller venue. Steinway Hall already existed, but was very small and mostly confined to piano recitals. The Aeolian Hall would shortly appear in New Bond Street, closer in size to Bechstein Hall, but based upon a pianola firm with less prestige. With an infrastructure at last in place, modern concert life could begin to take shape.

As the list of Bechstein 'fixtures' – they were so described in the office – was pencilled in, the annual count soon rose to some 200 concerts. May and June were the busiest months, mid-week afternoons at 3 pm and evenings at 8 pm the favourite times. Glancing at these early programmes one is tempted simply to pick out the stars. Some already well established names – Carreño, Joachim – are still familiar solely through the written word, but many newcomers were among the first generation of musicians to be satisfactorily captured for posterity by recording, and their sound is still familiar. Among them a few are instantly recognisable as 'defining' artists, of such influence that they imposed new repertoires, or styles and standards of performance. Most of this élite appeared at Bechstein Hall, many for their London debut. They figure large in these pages, for the Hall was undoubtedly their chosen platform, even if success sometimes took them to larger platforms. But the Hall's true significance in the history of London's music also demands a wider perspective. Attractive and open to anyone who could afford the modest hiring fee, Bechstein Hall inevitably became a mirror of contemporary music making, reflecting current tastes, ideas of programming, and levels of accomplishment, and, not least, contributing to their improvement. From the start, and increasingly over the first decade, each season included concerts at the highest level of technical, and occasionally artistic, achievement. But the obstacles to enlightenment were formidable. In contrast to many cities of continental Europe, London's market for music was not merely inordinately rich, but ruthlessly competitive and, lacking public subsidy or any substantial artistic patronage, notoriously 'commercial': many foreign musicians commented on this, in private. In such an environment it was impossible for a small venue to escape, particularly at first, the predominant culture of the Edwardian drawing-room.

Its flavour of gentility and a cultivated amateurishness is noticeable in the early years. Even today a visitor can take note of the Hall's rear entrance for 'ARTISTES'. Some programmes innocently portray their world. On 27 February 1903 at 8.30 pm, 'carriages at 10', Ulph Smith offers a 'musical and humorous recital', including God Save the King arranged in minuet style, and the Chopin A flat Ballade. On 14 May a 'morning concert' at 3 pm includes songs, a cellist, recitations and an American Humourist. A few days later Teresa del Riego, whose 'Homing' and 'Oh Dry those Tears' were best-sellers in the flourishing ballad market, lines up no less than twelve 'distinguished artists' to parade her wares. Publicity, recalling ancient styles touting for subscription, is elegantly printed to resemble a personal note in copperplate hand, to 'solicit your kind interest' and so forth. On June 8 at 8.15 pm carriages were not required until 10.30 for Anna Roeckner's Grand Evening Concert, which promised four vocalists, plus Lane-Wilson, a baritone who specialised in Olde Englishe Melodies, and two duologues, eventually replaced, with much Pooterish fuss, by a recitation. Such 'Grand Concerts', inciden-

Teresa del Riego's programme cover

BECHSTEIN HALL.

MISS

TERESA DEL RIEGO

BEGS TO ANNOUNCE HER SECOND

MATINÉE ✦ RECITAL

ON

Tuesday Afternoon, May 19th, 1903,

at 3 o'clock.

THE FOLLOWING DISTINGUISHED ARTISTS HAVE KINDLY CONSENTED TO ASSIST—

Miss Perceval Allen	Mr. C. Hayden-Coffin
Miss Martha Cunningham	Mr. Lawrence Rea
Mrs. Cleland Cornmell	Mr. Talleur Andrews

Mr. Maurice Farkoa.

Violin	-	Signor Arturo Tibaldi
Violoncello	-	Señor Rubio
Recitation	-	Miss Annie Hughes
At the Piano	-	Miss May Christie and
		Mr. Frank Lambert.

Sofa Stalls, 10/6;   Area, 5/-.;   Balcony, 2/6.

Tickets to be obtained from Miss TERESA DEL RIEGO, 53 Ladbroke Grove, Holland Park, W.; Messrs. CHAPPELL & Co., 50 New Bond Street and Box Office, Queen's Hall; Box Office, Bechstein Hall; and usual Agents.

tally, were already being openly derided by music critics, and never seriously reviewed. More exotic, but surely on a similar wavelength, was the appearance of Signor Jean Pietrapertosa 'solo mandolist to the Royal Courts of Italy and Belgium and Paris Grand Opera' who, with George Scalisi at the piano, played selections from his comic opera *Lady Mystery*. More celebrated, but similarly hard to place, were two appearances by the diseuse Yvette Guilbert. Hardly 'music at all', said *The Lady*, her art lay 'more in delineation of character than in actual singing . . . each song a little life drama.' And there were costume changes with every group. Homely pleasures returned when Karine Somers (Mrs Reg Somerville) and husband, were joined by Bertha Moore to recite and sing for the first time, in STORY AND SONG: 'The Nightingale and the Rose' from Oscar Wilde's collection *The Happy Prince*. A frequent visitor was Ernest Newlandsmith whose fulsome publicity boasted a long list of patrons headed by the Duke of Cambridge and His Serene Highness Prince Louis of Battenburg. And there's sartorial distinction: a mysterious photograph of the artiste outfitted in weird mediaeval kit as 'Laresol'. Evidently a cult figure, he played the violin, sometimes accompanied by 'the celebrated Newlandsmith string orchestra', in weirdly insubstantial programmes.

Recitals with more serious aspirations could challenge such insipidities, but even they had to contend with a culture where the typical programme was a ragbag attempting to please everybody with something. Only the most celebrated, or foolhardy, performer would risk appearing alone – in a venue with just a few hundred seats to be sold – without being 'assisted': that commonest of words in concert announcements. Singers would alternate with instrumentalists, 'heavy' music be followed by 'light' relief. A solo pianist would drop in with a couple of contrasted pieces, 'effective' or soulful. The young Percy Grainger, appearing so frequently and briefly that he was suspected of camping out near the Hall, would bound onto the platform, dispatch a Hungarian Rhapsody or Beethoven's 'The wrath over the lost farthing' (sic), and disappear as singer or string player returned. Violinists, novice or master, would almost always provide a concerto as centrepiece (the Tchaikovsky was currently favourite), with piano accompaniment. Boring bits, such as the opening tutti, would often be cut. The solo cello and its central literature were unknown territory, though Casals was beginning to change this in other venues.

More generally public and critical perception of an acknowledged repertoire was narrow and rigid to an extent inconceivable to the modern listener: with rare exceptions it consisted of a mere handful of works, even
when selected from 'the great masters'. Of Bach there was little, except
in 'hyphenated' piano arrangements, notably Busoni's; of earlier music
there was virtually nothing. Severely limited acquaintance with Mozart
and Schubert, and similarly modest assumptions about their stature, would
soon be upset by some marvellous initiatives. The general run of concerts
appears to have been put together for audiences with limited aspirations
or powers of concentration, no sense of incongruity or desire for coherence, less still an interest in comprehensiveness. And this was so even
with keyboard repertoire in the golden age of the piano. A performance
of Book One or Two of Bach's *Well-Tempered Clavier* would have been inconceivable, despite the organ loft's widespread influence, and umpteen
published treatises on fugue. An early visitor to the Hall who programmed the complete Preludes and Studies of everyone's favourite piano
composer earned reprimand and bewildered respect. Berthe Marx Gold-
schmidt's devotion of a whole recital to Chopin was reviewed as 'in itself
a doubtful scheme', its comprehensiveness 'certainly a mistake as regards
the Preludes', though the 'self-imposed task was carried out with courage
and energy.' It took half a century to move public expectations from
scrappiness to exhaustiveness, but Bechstein Hall, from the start, became
the most likely place for such challenge and innovation.

Inevitably the piano occupied centre stage, its connoisseurs – most
audiences then included a large proportion of amateur players – given
unprecedented opportunities, within a single year and continuously thereafter, to compare the contrasted styles of celebrities from every school
and to assess newcomers. Pachmann and Busoni were regular visitors with
diverse and generous programmes. One of the latter's consisted of Beethoven Sonata op. 110, the Brahms-Handel Variations, and four Schubert
Impromptus. Another: Beethoven op. 26; Fantasies by Schubert, 'The
Wanderer', and Liszt, on Donizetti's *Lucia*, and the Brahms-Paganini
Variations. Teresa Carreño, the Venezuelan 'Walküre of the piano', who
had studied with Anton Rubinstein and was approaching the end of a
magnificent career, stormed in with both of the Beethoven op. 27 Sonatas and an assortment of Chopin, Rubinstein and Liszt. The latter's dis-

tinguished Portuguese pupil, da Motta, gave four enormous 'historical' recitals; in one he included the *Waldstein* Sonata and Alkan's preposterous 'Concerto without Orchestra', and the culmination of his final programme was the Liszt Sonata, then rarely to be heard. The same master's Scottish pupil Frederic Lamond, already established as a leading Beethoven specialist, tackled similarly exhaustive programmes. Equally lavish and famously unique in technical command was Leopold Godowsky with Beethoven's Sonata *Les Adieux*, Brahms's Scherzo op. 4, three Mendelssohn 'Songs without words', his own *perpetuum mobile* arrangement of a Weber sonata movement, a Chopin Impromptu, Scherzo and Ballade, Liszt *Gnomenreigen*, and the Brahms Paganini Variations! That parade of keyboard masters, all associated with Bechstein pianos, could be heard within a few months, yet several novices also ventured to appear and were welcomed. Gertrude Peppercorn, a Matthay pupil like her contemporary Myra Hess, and fresh from success in Berlin, played a conventional but demanding recital to an 'overflowing audience'. *The Lady*'s astute critic noted that she displayed 'none of the coldness and angularity of most English pianists – a matter of congratulation when so many aspirants for

José Vianna da Motta   *Gertrude Peppercorn*

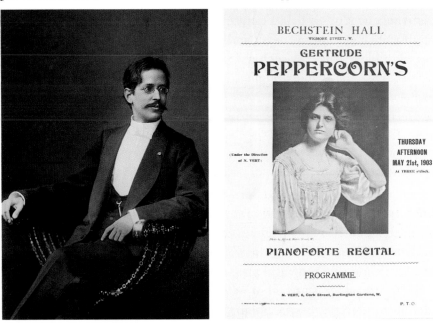

public fame hail from America and
the continent.' Similar enthusiasm
greeted the now forgotten Dorothy
Maggs who entered 'a crowded
Bechstein Hall' with the Brahms-
Handel Variations and 'a curious
Fantasie Orientale' by Balakirev (a
piece which later became familiar as
a touchstone of virtuosity). The
appearance of Frank Merrick, taught
(like Schnabel and Paderewski) by
Leschetizky and, that rare creature,
a significant Englishman on the platform, excited the *Morning Leader* to
exclaim, 'Great Britain is distinctly
looking up.' *The Lady* considered
him the best British pianist since
D'Albert and Lamond, adding 'the
priceless gift of thought' to the
familiar technical prowess expected
of his fellow pupils.

Frank Merrick's recital on 25 March 1903

Amidst this plethora one recital stands out in retrospect. A challenge
perceptible even to some contemporaries, it was England's first encoun-
ter with the most resolute and influential of 'defining' twentieth century
pianists. A few days after his successful debut in the Brahms second concerto at the Queen's Hall, Artur Schnabel arrived on 20 February, 1904, to
play early Beethoven, the Brahms Ballades op. 10, some Schumann and the
Schubert posthumous A major Sonata. This 'programme was certainly
out of the common, though lacking some great work which would test to
the full the intellectual and emotional powers of the newcomer' sniffed the
Athenaeum, with particular disdain for Schubert's 'weak development' and
outer movements of 'unjustifiable length'. By contrast, *The Times*, eccen-
trically anticipating later taste, welcomed 'one of the most beautiful sonatas
of all time', superb playing, and a demeanour 'unaffected and natural'.

That season, and for years to come, there was no comparable profusion and diversity in chamber music. An outstanding virtuoso might extend

perceptions of his instrument; as in May 1907 when Koussevitsky gave a recital on the double bass 'with artistic taste'. Famous violinists were usually content to appear with docile accompaniment, although celebrities sometimes played together: Godowsky joined Jacques Thibaud in the Brahms D minor and César Franck sonatas. Practised ensemble at the highest level only appeared on such rare occasions as a visit by the Moscow Trio: their programme included the trio by Tchaikovsky, most popular of symphonic composers. Rarest of all visitors was a first-class string quartet, with consequent neglect of that central repertoire. There were regular appearances by Hans Wessely's Quartet, then considered the best in England (with Spencer Dyke, Lionel Tertis, and Patterson Parker). A typical programme consisted of Beethoven op. 18 no. 1, the Grieg quartet and Brahms piano quintet with Gertrude Peppercorn. It is astonishing that even the Beethoven quartets, in stark contrast to his orchestral works, concertos and piano sonatas, were little known. A performance of op. 132 in November 1909 by the Klingler Quartet was reported as attracting a large audience because 'opportunities of hearing this great work are few and far between.' Yet the special occasion was still part of a mixed programme: the Brahms Quintet in G with Frank Bridge on viola, and a Schumann piano trio with Donald Tovey. At the highest level of playing and ensemble the Bohemian Quartet (Karel Hoffmann, Josef Suk, Oskar Nedbal, and Hanuš Wihan), on their first visit to the Hall in 1903, could claim to have been 'continuously associated for ten years.' That concert, of Dvořák, Beethoven and Nedbal, was warmly received, not only for superb playing, but for the appropriateness of venue, programming, and therefore audience. All this excited widespread comment because the Bohemian's recent appearance at another venue had been a disaster, with ruinous 'coming and going' by some members of the audience, presumably, it was said, attracted solely by some English songs on the programme, and allergic to string quartets. At a second Bechstein Hall concert the Bohemians responded to a warmly receptive audience with a coherent programme of Beethoven, Dvořák and Smetana. It was a useful lesson in concert promotion and a significant precedent.

If the Hall's greatest service over this formative decade was to extend the frontiers of musical understanding and enjoyment, then nothing could match its dissemination of Schubert and Mozart. At the start most of

Wessely Quartet on 2 March 1903   *Bohemian Quartet on 9 February 1903*

their chamber works were unknown to the public; and even critics were customarily indifferent to the occasional appearance of, say, the *Trout Quintet*. A handful of Lieder regularly appeared in mixed programmes, but no one – not even George Henschel to his own accompaniment, or the formidable team of Gerhardt and Nikisch – would venture anything approaching a Schubertiad. It was therefore a symbolic achievement, a generation ahead of its time, when Zur-Mühlen, on 4 June 1903, accompanied by Conrad von Bos, sang Schubert's *The Beautiful Miller-Maid*. This cycle was 'seldom given in its entirety', twittered the word book with absurd understatement. Priced at sixpence it includes the German words, a brief description (not translation) in English of each song, and a preface in German by Oxford Professor Max Müller, son of the poet. Comparably ground-breaking was the appearance, in June 1910, of the 74-year-old Saint-Saëns with a small hand-picked orchestra to perform ten Mozart piano concertos, mostly with his own cadenzas. They were grouped as follows: K503, 413, 453 and 488; K595, 537 and 491; K271, 467, 450 (the audience was reminded that he had played this in 1846 at the age of ten) and 466. All of these now familiar masterpieces were new to his audience, with the possible exception of 466 and 491, and still hard to accept. *The Times* was gratified to hear 'the eminent composer (Saint-Saëns) give out some simple theme that in less sympathetic hands would be full of banality.' The *Athenaeum* acknowledged that the concertos were 'little known' and 'regarded by many as excellent specimens', but they had been 'surpassed' by 'Beethoven, and still more by Schumann, Liszt and Tchaikovsky.' The 'pianoforte writing is not difficult enough to interest most pianists, and not exciting enough to satisfy the public.' Small orchestras were often accommodated by extending the platform, on payment of an extra two guineas, sufficiently, said the management, to 'hold with ease 40 players.' On 2 November 1906 a newcomer 'dispensed with score and also baton', showing 'marked ability as a conductor, his excellent orchestra of 34 just the right size for eighteenth century music.' Mr Thomas Beecham's eccentric programme, evidently unfamiliar to the critics, included a 'delightful novelty' by Mozart, Symphony no. 38, 'The Prague'.

Throughout 1913, the last year of peace and sanity, London was overwhelmed by music, much of it new or magnificent, or both, a plethora beyond wildest imagining. Most spectacular were the Russian Ballet and Chaliapin's Boris; plentiful Wagner (for his centenary) including three *Ring* cycles under Nikisch and several in English; Beecham conducting *Der Rosenkavalier* (new to England) and *Ariadne*; Melba and Caruso in *La Bohème*; Beecham again with a new orchestra on Sundays at the Palladium (*sic*) returning from triumphant performances in Berlin. The total number of London concerts was 'making the head swim' complained the *Daily Telegraph* in mid-season, reviewing fifty a week plus opera. And 61 Proms were to come, in themselves a season 'by far the most prosperous ever yet enjoyed' concluded the *Annual Register*. Night after night Queen's Hall 'was literally packed by enthusiasts.' Bechstein Hall was now offering some 300 concerts, including a fair share of illustrious names. The singers included Gerhardt – usually heard in larger venues – Vladimir Rosing with fashionable Russian songs, and Yvette Guilbert. And there was Lula Mysz-Gmeiner whose English première of Mahler's *Kindertotenlieder* was

"He is a conductor of remarkable ability.' —*The Times*.

THE . . .

THOMAS BEECHAM

Orchestral

Concerts. .

Mr. THOMAS BEECHAM begs to announce

Four
Orchestral Concerts

AT

BECHSTEIN HALL

ON

FRIDAY,	NOVEMBER 2nd, 1906,	at 8.30 p.m.
WEDNESDAY,	NOVEMBER 21st, 1906,	at 8.30 p.m.
WEDNESDAY,	DECEMBER 12th, 1906,	at 8.30 p.m.
WEDNESDAY,	JANUARY 23rd, 1907,	at 8.30 p.m.

(Under the management of Mr. LESLIE HIBBERD-)

The Orchestra, specially selected for these concerts, will consist of a picked body of players drawn from the best London Permanent Orchestras.

Sofa Stalls, 7/6;   Area Stalls (Reserved), 5/- ;   Balcony (Unreserved), 2/6
Subscription Tickets for the Series—Sofa Stalls, 25/-;   Area Stalls, 15/-;   Balcony, 7/6.

To be obtained at the Box Office, Bechstein Hall: of Chappell & Co., Ltd., 50 New Bond Street and Box Office, Queen's Hall; Army & Navy Stores, 105 Victoria Street, Westminster, S.W.; Lacon & Ollier; Ashton; Mitchell; Hays; Keith, Prowse, & Co., Ltd. (all Branches); Webster & Waddington, Ltd., 304 Regent Street, W.; Cecil Roy, 15 Sussex Place, 11 Pont Street, S.W., Albert Gate, Gloucester Road, and 59 South Audley Street; Leader & Co.; Webster & Girling, 44 Upper Baker Street; at Box Office, Steinway Hall; the usual Agents; and of

LESLIE HIBBERD, 17 Hanover Square, W,
Tel. 5387 Gerr.

Announcement for Thomas Beecham's concerts

condemned by *The Times* for its 'depressing monotony', in contrast to her welcome Wolf songs. Pianists continued to predominate: Busoni, da Motta, Lamond and Pachmann ('some went to hear his comments and see his gestures'), and Arthur Rubinstein, returning after a successful debut in the previous year. Significant newcomers included Egon Petri, Katherine Goodson and 'a remarkable girl' Guiomar Novaes, 'find of the season', who was already being compared to Carreño (Lucy Broadwood was in the audience and organised a party for her). A barely noticed Edwin Fischer accompanied a singer and played some Bach. Despite Busoni's continued influence, it was becoming increasingly common for a recitalist to play a little unhyphenated Bach: Myra Hess offered some of the 48, and Harold Bauer such 'unfamiliar' works as the C minor Toccata.

The Hall's line-up of chamber music was also beginning to extend and improve. Violinists proliferated, sometimes with serious intent; some cellists, including Beatrice Harrison and Felix Salmond, followed Casals's

Myra Hess

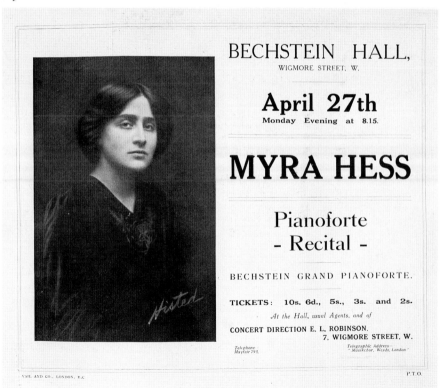

lead by attending to their instrument's basic repertoire; and there were more, occasionally better, string quartets. Home-grown ensembles, in addition to the Wessely, included the English String Quartet and, probably rather better, the London String Quartet. Albert Sammons, Thomas Petre, H. Waldo Warner and Warwick Evans had been playing together since 1910, their leader a self-taught cockney without formal education who had been talent-spotted by Beecham playing at the Waldorf Hotel. Punctilious in rehearsal, the London players were already programming such recent works as the quartets of Debussy and Dohnányi (1906). Most celebrated of visitors were Vienna's Rosé Quartet, founded in 1882, and New York's Flonzaley, established in 1903. The latter performed Schoenberg's D minor Quartet, and those who expected 'weird noises', reported the *Telegraph*, were grievously disappointed, for it was well-ordered, intelligent and occasionally ravishing but inordinately long. Generally the year's programmes still included lacklustre events – loosely packaged recitals, debuts which ended a career, 'pupils' concerts' fit only for families and friends – but the overall impression is one of increasing sophistication and a sense of direction, even a certain rigour.

It had already become a common conceit among weary journalists to question the musicality of Londoners presented with this surfeit of music. 'Efforts to create audiences are useless here,' declared the *Telegraph*; and the *Monthly Musical Record* was similarly convinced that the 'public has little conception of style or period in music', contrasting what happened at concerts with the coherence of display in an art gallery. But Bechstein Hall could generally escape such animadversions because of its reputation for professionalism and quality. Most bookings, particularly in high season, were now long-term commitments and therefore less easily secured by the novice or nondescript. But despite obvious advantages of location and prestige, this degree of success was ultimately dependent upon management which, since 1905, had been in the capable hands of William John Kirkby Pearson. A Yorkshireman, educated in Battersea and married to the prominent singer Louise Kirkby Lunn, Pearson had acquired adequate familiarity with music and musicians, along with the business acumen, tact and common sense essential for concert management. He also practised the more elusive, dedicated skills of an 'enabler', crucial to success in the market-driven anarchy of London music. In a typical week he would persuade Beecham to audition a promising young singer, and fix the studio arrangements; advise Lamond to change a forthcoming Bechstein date which threatened to clash with Rosenthal at Queen's Hall (to mutual loss); inform newly visiting artists about local transport facilities and instruct them in the all-important mysteries of advertising and how to handle critics; cope with a customer's complaint, and another's request for preferential or complimentary seats . . . and so forth. No detail was too slight, no correspondent too humble or lofty for considerate and firm response. Audiences, artists and agents everywhere were thus encouraged to regard Bechstein Hall as *the* London place for serious music on a small scale. Then, quite suddenly, things fell apart.

§ *Dropping the name and keeping the place.* When war began in August 1914 Bechstein, like all German businesses in Britain, was put into the hands of an official 'Receiver and Manager'. But the Hall, after a brief period of uncertainty which affected all places of entertainment, opened again under Pearson who characteristically established cordial working relations with the Receiver: subsequent events and surviving correspondence in the Bechstein archive confirm this significant fact. Many bookings were cancelled, of course, and the collapse of international travel inevitably affected the variety and quality of surviving concerts, but such artists as Moiseiwitsch and Myra Hess maintained standards and drew large audiences. The availability and use of Bechstein pianos was not yet in question: indeed when a Professor Lillo Saito requested twelve (*sic*), for an event with string orchestra in October 1915, the only response was to ask about disposition between grands and uprights to fit the stage. In addition to individual recitals there were concerts for the Belgian Refugees Appeal and similar charities, and numerous patriotic meetings addressed by such luminaries as John Buchan. Therefore application to the London County Council for renewal of the Hall's licence in November 1915 was presumably expected to be a normal and uneventful routine. This did not allow for the activities of a professional patriot.

The Pianomaker was a downmarket trade paper, ignored by the best pianomakers of all countries, whose editor engaged in a mean and philistine rant to impress the lower reaches of the English industry in competition with German firms. By 1916 the rhetoric, which now seems comic in its excess, suddenly became all too appropriate, his savaging of Bechstein Hall a minuscule but representative skirmish in a year notorious for obscene carnage and futility. Leading musicians, 'crowned heads' and high society were favourite targets: Melba for singing 'Land of Hope and Glory' accompanied on a Bechstein; Moiseiwitsch simply for playing in the Hall, though his Russian blouse earned approval. Heroic efforts to 'squash the Bechstein business' were intended to culminate in the 'internment' and 'deportation' of all their pianos. Scenting a kill the editor therefore converted the licence application into a great battle, employing King's Counsel to argue that renewal would be ruinous to the nation since the Hall was 'simply used as an advertising medium for getting rid of German goods in this country.' The battle was won, the licence refused. An appeal against this decision was led by Berridge, the official Receiver and colleague of Pearson, who reported the Hall's war record – even Sir Edward Grey had lectured there – and insisted that no remnant of German control remained, nor was there any risk that so much as a farthing could be sent to Germany. The appeal failed and in November 1916 everything was auctioned – Hall, studios, offices, furniture including 137 fine pianos, and a remunerative tuning connection; available for sale to 'anyone not under foreign influence'. The nearby shop Debenham and Freebody, without musical credentials, acquired the lot for £56,500: quite a bargain, since the Hall alone had cost £100,000 to build, in pre-war pounds, and the pound had since halved in value. The celebrating victors reported that henceforth only English instruments would be stocked – as good as or better than Bechsteins – and some believed there would be a drive 'to make the Debenham piano the finest on the market.'

In similar language the future of the Hall was also assumed to be secure. 'Without any fuss', announced the *Musical Times*, discreetly ignoring the loss of name and image, 'this convenient hall was reopened on January 16. The new designation is a happy one because it at once declares where the Hall is to be found.' But few concert-goers found mere location a sufficient attraction when Sammons and Safonov inaugurated the renamed Wigmore Hall with the first of three Beethoven sonata recitals. Whatever the violinist's sterling qualities, they were an ill-matched pair, and Safonov's subsequent replacement by William Murdoch did little to boost attendance. Far more interesting was a farewell appearance in July by 'the clever boy pianist known as Solomon' who was retiring 'for a time to study in repose.' Meanwhile the indomitable Pearson set about rebuilding custom and goodwill, while coping not only with the exigencies of war, but also with a new burden of paperwork from the recently created Performing Right Society. Bravely he promised one correspondent that the public 'will once again cheerfully go to evening concerts as the Air Defences are now so excellent'; reminded several that management and 'artistic purposes' were unchanged, except for free choice of (British and Allied) pianos; organised safe accommodation for the congregation of the Liberal Jewish Synagogue – gratefully ack-

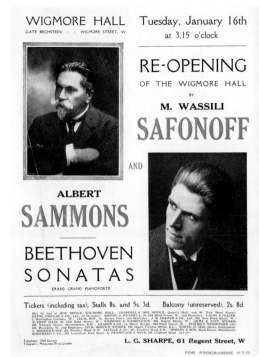

Sammons and Safonoff, 16 January 1917

nowledged in most illiberal times; even assured Baring Brothers, in an attempt to book a recital by the immensely popular violinist Marie Hall, that 'the quality of concerts given is rapidly approaching the old pre-war standard.' If the latter claim was glossed, what could be done was being done to repair and reactivate. John Ireland, for example, was given elaborate guidance to the role of advertising – 'not so much to bring the people in as to leave no excuse for the absence of the critics' – and its placement, including the precise allocation of billboards and sandwich-board men. And there were occasional reminders of pre-war achievements. Thus when Tertis gave a viola recital in December 1917 it was not merely a rare opportunity for the instrument but another significant extension of repertoire with what was described as 'a Mozart concertante for violin and viola' (K364) – with piano accompaniment.

The Armistice left a residue of commitments: to reassure the Navy and Army Canteen Board that 'a good clean interesting entertainment' could be provided for free troop concerts; to promise an aristocratic fusspot and very military lecturer the assistance of 'an experienced lanternist with the necessary collapsible screen.' There was even some music, from Moiseiwitsch, though now burdened by an uncharacteristic hardness of tone: surely due to an inadequate piano, said the busy critic William Atheling, otherwise known as Ezra Pound, in a comment which would have been inconceivable before the war. More enthusiasm was lavished upon Vladimir Rosing, particularly in Mussorgsky songs, but what were listeners to make of his politically correct Schumann? 'J'ai pardonné' could eventually be identified as 'Ich grolle nicht', which was at least preferable, thought Pound, to 'I do not growl'. In 1920 Rosing was still singing Brahms in French, but when he asked an audience if they object-ed to Schumann in German, there were loud cries of 'No' and warm applause. *The Lady* approved: 'Now that we have defeated the enemy and are at peace with him, we ought not to keep up a boycott of German lyrics.' Meanwhile standards were being re-established by a few instru-mentalists, to spectacular effect with the violin. One afternoon in May 1920 Heifetz 'outstripped everyone in mastery' at the Queen's Hall, while

Huberman was in the Wigmore, 'occasional blemishes' serving 'only to throw into relief the great beauty' of his Bach. Next month perfection in chamber music was attributed to the Flonzaley, 'a perfection so severe', pronounced the customarily rigorous *Athenaeum*, 'that there are few quar-tets good enough for them to play. Mozart alone came through their trial unscathed', not so Loeffler and Smetana. The same austerity graded a new cello concerto, with some pre-cision when it was performed by Beatrice Harrison, with York Bowen at the piano: 'About 65% of it is really good Elgar' but 'there are things here and there that are rank bad.' A year earlier (21 May 1919)

Harrison and Bowen, 29 May 1920

WIGMORE HALL,
WIGMORE STREET, W.

MAY, MARGARET,
AND
BEATRICE

HARRISON

RECITAL

Saturday, May 29th, at 3

Assisted by

YORK BOWEN.

CHAPPELL GRAND PIANOFORTE.

Telephone—3156 Mayfair.
Telegrams—"Organd, Wesdo, London."

Under the direction of Messrs. IBBS & TILLETT,
19 Hanover Square, W.1.

the 65% achiever had been present in person for first performances of his String Quartet and Piano Quintet, and the Violin Sonata played by Sammons and Murdoch.

Throughout the war, said Pound, there had been 'so little major piano playing in London' that 'critical machinery' had rusted. But now Lamond was back, 'the real thing, the old style *maestro* in full command of his instrument', drawing an attentive audience. And a new style *maestro* consolidated his pre-war reputation with three recitals which ranged from the Liszt sonata, Chopin preludes and Schumann symphonic studies to a Vivaldi concerto (with trimmings), Franck, and complete Debussy preludes. Alfred Cortot's playing was pronounced 'unequalled in peculiar characteristics of texture.' Then back to the old masters with Busoni making his 'rentrée' with a selection of Goldberg Variations (*sic*, in his own arrangement) and the *Hammerklavier*: 'One of the marvels of the age' enthused *The Lady*, who 'makes us understand what people felt when they listened to the Abbé Liszt.' Privately the great man was ill at ease, complaining to his wife about being forced to use a poor instrument while 'in the showrooms which were formerly Bechstein's there are twenty-five beautiful pianos . . . and one is not allowed to play on them! Is it not mad!' Yet, as he observed to a pupil, banishing these instruments from public platforms did not prevent the few on sale from being 'only too eagerly bought up' for private use.

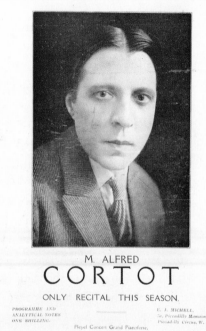

Alfred Cortot, 22 November 1919

Throughout the 1920s occasional good music at Wigmore Hall threw into sharp relief the decade's prevailing mediocrity. Orchestral concerts were notoriously ill-disciplined and unrehearsed, even at Queen's Hall, and the smaller venues were so flooded by incompetence as to provoke widespread reaction from those forced to attend. It was actually a Wigmore recital which never rose 'above mediocrity' that ignited the *Athenaeum's* blaze of indignation against a 'perfect army of musical purveyors . . . singers in their thousands, pianists in their tens of thousands' who 'step forward onto the platform of the Wigmore Hall or the Aeolian presumably for our benefit since it is not, apparently for their own.' Many were 'deficient alike in intellect and in technique', and their 30% audience probably 'half paper' (free tickets). *The Lady,* customarily gentler in response, could not but agree that far 'too many immature artists appear in public,' but found a solution in market economics, 'the weeding out process accomplishes itself automatically . . . only the fit survive.' Another journal's much quoted attack on 'The Recital Scandal' blamed agents, teachers (touting pupils) and even complacent reviewers for a ridiculous surfeit of would-be performers in excess of any possible audience. Protests rumbled on throughout the decade to no effect, for there was no limit to those who could afford to appear, either through honestly naïve aspiration, or simply to boast of a London appearance.

By 1928 the *Spectator* was still trying to explain the logic of a pernicious market. Lack of genuine demand led to 'papering' and the assembling of audiences which, 'particularly in the vicinity of Oxford Circus' were notorious for their lack of initiative, genuine desire for music, character, spirit, or even 'ordinary decent manners.' Managers were not to blame for it was their task to hire out a hall 'to a renowned Lieder singer on one night', then to novices and 'Bohemian' entertainments, and finally to 'a suburban restaurant trio.' Wigmore lettings fit that pattern, passively accepting all comers and filling the diary. If annual proceeds satisfactorily averaged £4,000 to £5,000, a decent return on the 1917 investment, there was scant regard for artistic consistency or regaining the prestige once attached to the Hall. Fleeting visits by interesting newcomers and established artists might temporarily improve the image, notably so in 1923. The reclusive pianist Youra Guller gave two recitals: she would reappear fifty years later, revered but still obscure. In nice contrast was the debut of a brilliant violin prodigy whose birth certificate could be 'verified in the vestibule' to belie a 'mature appearance.' The Bruch Concerto, Tartini 'Devil's Trill' and some Bach launched Alfredo

Campoli's unique career. The Bohemian Quartet returned, and the Léner Quartet were greeted with acclaim. Their first recital (Brahms A minor, Ravel, Haydn op. 76 no. 5) was immediately followed by another, and an extra 'by special request'. A month later they were back again and, in November, yet again, clearly responding to a thirst for high achievement in a culture of isolated events and scant or ill-focussed promotion. Janáček's visit in 1926, for example, was hardly noticed and further obscured by the General Strike. In 1927 Landowska made a rare appearance, playing harpsichord and piano, while Segovia gave two recitals, followed by a hastily fixed third.

Then, in the wider world of the late twenties, there began a sequence of disruption and innovation which transformed the world of music and entertainment irrevocably. Talkies replaced silent films practically overnight, creating a new all-powerful entertainment industry, and destroying the principal means of employment for instrumentalists everywhere, along with bonfires of sheet music which alarmed the publishers. Electricity transformed radio, records and their repertoire, with the position of London consequently reinforced as a major centre for music. Meanwhile the old-established structure of the music industry and music making was being torn apart, by sudden collapse (of the pianola boom) and by long-term but precipitating erosion (of piano ownership and lessons, now ceasing to be obligatory). Music in the home was undergoing a sea change from playing and singing at the piano to listening to gramophone and wireless. While most of these interrelated events affected music in every country, the British enjoyed two singular benefits: a London-based record industry with a stake in serious music and, *mirabile dictu*, Reith's BBC, armed with unprecedented public funding and dedicated to the nation's enlightenment.

All this happened before the 1930s slump and general depression. But in music, if the 1920s were a decade of profusion and a preponderance of the second-rate, the 1930s advanced steadily in the opposite direction, with immense benefit to discriminating audiences. In addition to forming the country's first stable, trained and rehearsed symphony orchestra, the BBC rescued Queen's Hall (and therefore the Proms) and launched a tremendous programme of music and education, including public concerts with close attention to the avant-garde. The record companies became

Léner Quartet, 15 March 1923   *Segovia, 31 May 1927*

worthy allies to similar purpose, rapidly building a 'standard repertoire'
– even in chamber music – of exemplary performances by such artists as
Schnabel, the Busch Quartet and Gerhard Hüsch. Opportunities for repeated listening thus made a formidably new contribution to understanding, and the desire for 'difficult' music in live performance. The Wigmore
Hall gained from this renaissance, reflected its achievements, and within
its financial straitjacket was sometimes able to make a positive contribution. Thus a 'co-operative' of well-known singers and players announced
that their Wednesday evening concerts would attempt to 'make the general public acquainted with chamber music.' One concert was devoted to
Bach, another by Myra Hess and Harold Samuel to duet sonatas by Mozart
and Brahms; at another Plunket Greene sang Schumann's *Dichterliebe*.
The *Spectator* found performances and audiences 'both intelligent and
enthusiastic . . . no foolish demands for repetitions and no signs of aloof
highbrow appraisement.' When Hess, D'Arányi and Salmond played piano
trios by Mozart, Brahms and Schubert, *The Times* reported a characteris-

tic example of everyone's involvement: the misfortune of a broken cello string was 'turned to pleasure by the two ladies reminding each other (and the audience) of other good things of Brahms while they waited for the mending.' A few weeks later Adolf Busch and Rudolf Serkin in Mozart, Brahms and the Schubert Fantasie 'made listeners share in the tingling life of the music.'

By 1933, with a new manager, Harry Brickell (appointed in 1932), there were many programmes of distinction, along with surviving elements of tosh. The School of Wisdom, incorporating the Institute of Efficology, was inaugurated with an address on 'the necessity of Wisdom' and music by Arensky and Chopin: admission only by personal invitation. The general public, however, could attend six concerts by the Busch Quartet and Serkin, including all three Brahms violin sonatas. Programmes now significantly carried advertisements for the relevant gramophone records. For the Brahms centenary, no less than eight concerts were devoted to his complete chamber music – 25 works played by ten artists including Isolde Menges and Harold Samuel – a kind of celebration common enough to us, but quite extraordinary then. The London String Quartet, now with Primrose as viola, devoted four concerts to all of the Beethoven quartets after op. 18: another gesture towards unaccustomed completeness. And there was Szigeti with Bloch and solo Bach. In such ways did high seriousness mirror the times, and the growing presence of refugees from Germany, on stage and in the auditorium. In 1934 it becomes almost commonplace for critics to commend both artists and audiences as exemplary, in stark contrast to their reports of a decade before. The Busch are playing, with Serkin their 'perfect 5th', and audiences 'listen with the keenness that is a kind of participation': surely the ultimate accolade. Artists 'make their audience', concludes the *Musical Times*, exulting in an experience which included the Brahms Horn Trio with Aubrey Brain, the *Trout* Quintet, and Frank Bridge's G minor String Quartet. More equivocal are the comments on a well-intentioned 'Festival of English Chamber Music' in March 1936. The music itself, described as by 'established composers' and newcomers, excites no more than the comment (and this was a sympathetic writer) that patrons 'cannot create genius.' But there was curiosity about the audiences, apparently large, since admission was free, and disturbingly 'peripatetic'. More of an occasion was a memorial concert by the Roth Quartet in October dedicated to the munificent – all too rare but now forgotten – patron Edward Speyer. Soon after there was Milstein's Vivaldi and Bach; then Lili Krauss and Simon Goldberg with Bach, Mozart, Beethoven and Debussy.

Even those splendours are excelled by the extraordinary lavishness of 1938, a wondrous Spring of chamber music. First came the New Hungarian Quartet, including Sándor Végh, and bringing Bartók's 5th Quartet, welcomed as 'more genial' than most of his work. Then the Busch returned with four monumental concerts: one programme consisting simply of the first Rasoumovsky and Schubert G major Quartets. In May it was the Budapest Quartet's turn with Haydn op. 77 in G, Mozart 'Dissonance' and Beethoven op. 133 with the Grosse Fuge. In November Rudolph Dolmetsch ('the musical one' as a carping critic once remarked) steered unaccustomed members of the London Symphony Orchestra through some Albinoni, Picchi, and Bach's Musical Offering, which the programme described ('grimly', as the *Musical Times* observed) as a 'Musical Sacrifice' to a great cause.

World War II, like its predecessor, began with official stifling of music: all public concerts were stopped for three weeks. And when they were allowed to begin again the great initiative came, of course, from Myra Hess at the National Gallery, teaching audiences, as the *Spectator*'s critic remarked, the 'virtues of brevity, cheapness and absence of frills.' Meanwhile, for several seasons, the Wigmore was housing such efforts as an ENSA string orchestra's 'pleasant afternoon's music, adequately played.' But in 1943 it provided a platform for revolution. On 17 July Walter Goehr conducted Tippett's Concerto for Double String Orchestra in which Edward Sackville-West discerned 'the prophetic quality one finds in the best of Shostakovich . . . the brilliant, merciless, confident eye of a new musical age.' The *New Statesman* critic came to the Hall in October for the Lennox Berkeley Divertimento and a serenade by Benjamin Britten for tenor and horn, his 'most recent and best work . . . one would have to go some way back in time, and to some other country to find music of such astonishing imaginative scope and dramatic power.' The work 'bode well for Britten's future as a composer of operas.' In the *Observer* William Glock concluded a long and detailed review by urging the BBC to 'see that the country is made aware of its new masterpiece.' Even the *Spectator*

WIGMORE HALL

1940's?
1943

MUSICAL CULTURE LIMITED PRESENTS
TWO ORCHESTRAL CONCERTS

SATURDAYS at 2.45

June 19

GLINKA:	Kamarinskaya
KNIPPER:	Lyric Suite
SHOSTAKOVITCH:	Two Pieces for Strings *(First Performance in England)*
VEPRIK:	Five Orchestral Pieces *(First Performance in England)*
MOUSSORGSKY:	Introduction to Act I "Khovantschina"
TCHAIKOVSKY:	Suite No. 1 (Op. 43)

THIS CONCERT IS UNDER THE AUSPICES OF THE SOCIETY FOR CULTURAL RELATIONS WITH THE U.S.S.R.

July 17

BERLIOZ:	The Flight into Egypt (Overture, Part II, "The Childhood of Christ")
HAYDN:	Trumpet Concerto
WOLF:	Songs with Orchestra
TIPPETT:	Concerto for Double String Orchestra *(First Performance)*
FAURE:	"Dolly" Suite

VICTOR CARNE (Solo Tenor)

GEORGE ESKDALE (Solo Trumpet)

WALTER GOEHR

and concert ensemble led by Maria Lidka

Tickets: 7/6, 5/-, 2/6 from Box Office Wigmore Hall, W.1
(Telephone : WELbeck 2141)

First performance of Tippett's Concerto for Double String Orchestra, 17 July 1943 grumpily acknowledged an 'enormous cleverness.' At another concert promoted by Boosey and Hawkes in May 1944 there was Honegger and the Berg Lyric Suite, but the 'piece which had evidently caused the hall to be packed to overflowing (chiefly with quite young people)' was again the Serenade, with Peter Pears and Dennis Brain giving a 'performance of incredible virtuosity.' It was 'good news that this exquisite and profound work is to be recorded with the soloists for whom it was written.' A month earlier there was another evening of exquisite profundity, definitive English music making which would also later be recorded for posterity: Clifford Curzon playing a Schubert Impromptu and the Sonata in D; Pears and Britten in *Die schöne Müllerin*. And that magnificent year's

WIGMORE HALL, W.1

SCHUBERT RECITAL

CLIFFORD CURZON   PETER PEARS   BENJAMIN BRITTEN

Programme

IMPROMPTU IN G FLAT, OP. 90, No. 3

SONATA IN D, OP. 53

Allegro vivace
Con moto
SCHERZO : Allegro vivace
RONDO : Allegro moderato

CLIFFORD CURZON

INTERVAL

SONG CYCLE : DIE SCHÖNE MÜLLERIN, OP. 25

PETER PEARS and BENJAMIN BRITTEN

(1)   *WANDERING*

To wander is the miller's joy,
To wander.
A foolish miller he must seem,
Who never wanders by his stream.

And so we have our lesson learnt,
From water.
It knows no rest by night or day,
But wanders on its own sweet way.

To wander wander is my joy,
To wander !
O master keep me not at home,
But let me ever freely roam
And wander.

(2)   *WHITHER ?*

I heard a brooklet gushing
From out its rocky spring,
As down the valley rushing
So sweetly did it sing.

I know not how it happened,
Nor why I chose this path,
But I must hurry downward
Upon my faithful staff.

Still downward and ever onward
And ever beside the stream,
Which murmured still more sweetly
And ever clearer did seem.

Is this the way before me ?
O whither, brooklet say ?
You have with your soft murmur
Quite charmed my sense away.

Is this the brooklet's murmur ?
This can no murmur be.
The water nymphs are singing
A magic melody.

Sing on then, my friend, beside me,
And wander at your will,
A millwheel's always turning
In every sparkling rill.

Programme Sixpence

Sunday, 30th April, 1944

IBBS & TILLETT, 124 WIGMORE STREET, W.1

Curzon, Pears and Britten recital, 30 April 1944

achievements included Gerald Cooper's chamber concerts which defied the flying bombs, and Boyd Neel's orchestra playing Stravinsky's *Apollo*. An accolade was bestowed by Shawe-Taylor 'deeply grateful for these attempts to break away from the monotony of our wartime concert fare.'

On 22 November 1945 one concert covered 'a little cluster of anniversaries': Purcell's death, Britten's birth (he was performing at the concert) and St Cecilia's Day. A 'handful of our best young musicians' performed Britten's second quartet, the Donne Sonnets, and Purcell songs with accompaniments 'realised' from the thoroughbass. By the time Margaret Ritchie, Peter Pears and Richard Wood had reached the secular songs 'the concert had long since ceased to be a memorial occasion and had become as much an orgy of unrestrained enjoyment as Tchaikovsky in B flat minor at the Albert Hall.' The reference to South Kensington is poignant because orchestral concerts had recently been banished to its echoing wastes when Queen's Hall was destroyed in an air raid. Bereft of its lifelong companion and rival, the Wigmore Hall had survived, with acoustic, platform, and sometimes audience, unrivalled. 'Now that incuriosity and indifference to quality have become the rule among our audiences, there is an encouraging quality about the little Wigmore Hall public,' wrote Shawe-Taylor, '. . . critical, curious and alert, they know a good thing when they hear it.' They were also – they had to be – hair-shirted and robust, even by the standards of an austere generation. The newly formed Arts Council was now taking over, and a confidential memo observed the outcome of penny-pinching neglect: 'The Wigmore audience has got accustomed to the squalor of its surroundings and to discomfort.' No seats had been replaced since 1900 and all were now beyond repair; lighting, similarly untouched, was 'totally unsatisfactory'; extensive cleaning and decorating would be essential 'to keep the place respectable.' A little public money was at last being allocated to music, and therefore minimal repairs could be undertaken. But the Council was, of course, merely a landlord, balancing the books without much concern for artistic direction.

For the next few years the Hall was easily hired out to a host of newcomers and artists resuming their careers after the long break of war. Some added lustre, none more so than Dinu Lipatti on 4 April 1948. He did not so much play the piano, wrote Martin Cooper, as allow it to sound, *sonare*, and the tragic lustre of that sound – Chopin's B minor Sonata, a

Liszt Petrarch Sonnet, and the Ravel *Alborada del Gracioso* – survives on record as indelible proof of perfection. More frequent, but no less significant a turning-point in their assertion of absolute excellence and, in this case, post-war English musicality, were concerts by the Amadeus Quartet. After a performance on 26 May 1950 Paul Hamburger explained the reasons for this new group's international standing: 'Perfect unity of intention and spaciousness of conception.' On that occasion they played Mozart's Quartet K387 and the Schubert Octet, with Dennis Brain, John Alexandra, Frederick Thurston and Edward Merrett. In such company the critic was moved to quote Thomas Mann: 'Music is ennobled Time.' Comparable exultation attended Wilhelm Kempff's belated London debut on 27 October 1951 which included Beethoven op. 111 and the Schubert B flat Sonata. The artist was long familiar from recordings, the Hall packed with connoisseurs. Yet, despite such occasional burnishings of image and a permanently unmatched acoustic, there was probably a lurking suspicion, at least in the Arts establishment, that its best days were over. Lettings were falling from the immediate post-war peak; worn-out carpets and central heating would soon have to be replaced. Aspirations for concert life now centred upon a brave new, fresh as paint, South Bank world: in 1951 with the Royal Festival Hall, in 1967 the Queen Elizabeth Hall, and subsequently the Purcell Room, providing increasing and seemingly overwhelming competition for the old place. Already in 1954 there was an official desire 'to find business houses who might like to take the Wigmore Hall for their AGMs or similar occasions', they 'could have drinks and a cinema projector'. A few artists kept coming – in that same year *The Times* reviewed three harpsichord recitals by

Wilhelm Kempff recital, 27 October 1951

WIGMORE HALL
WIGMORE STREET   ·   ·   ·   W.I

ONLY RECITAL THIS SEASON
BY THE FAMOUS PIANIST

WILHELM

KEMPFF

SATURDAY, OCTOBER 27 at 7.30
1951

STEINWAY PIANOFORTE

TICKETS (INC. TAX): Reserved 9/- and 6/-   Unreserved 3/-
(All bookable in advance)
May be obtained from BOX OFFICE, WIGMORE HALL, (WELbeck 2141), usual Ticket Offices and
IBBS & TILLETT Ltd., 124 WIGMORE STREET, W.I
Ticket Office : Welbeck 8418   Hours : 10-5 ; Saturday 10-12

(1951)   FOR PROGRAMME P.T.O.

the outstanding Scarlatti authority Ralph Kirkpatrick, which provided unprecedented opportunity for the 'acquaintance of a composer who has hitherto been rather a shadowy figure.' And some debuts mattered. On 1 March 1961 a 16-year-old girl launched her newly acquired Stradivarius cello into the Brahms E minor and Debussy sonatas, a Bach suite and Falla's Spanish songs. Her great teacher, William Pleeth, and agent Emmie Tillett, had ensured a sold-out knowledgeable audience for Jacqueline du Pré. But such talent and promotion were rare and the Hall's future seemed very bleak.

Meanwhile public conceptions of repertoire and performance styles were being thoroughly shaken up, largely by long-playing records and broadcasts. Unlimited extension was the keynote. Music newly made accessible to the public was extended particularly to compositions before Bach, but also more generally to absolute completeness with major composers, and ceaseless explorations elsewhere. And there were associated changes in the content, presentation and packaging of live music. A set of pieces would necessarily be delivered whole rather than piecemeal; the great song cycles and exhaustive surveys of instrumental works became common fare, as did the entire output of minor and allegedly neglected composers. String soloists no longer played concertos with piano accompaniment, and many programmes were devised with a rigour which would have surprised Schnabel. Most spectacular was the ascent of 'Early Music', a multiplicity of new groups, many of them English, attracting new, keen, predominantly young audiences. Very much a movement or cult, its disciples were particularly concerned to reinstate old instruments – recorders, baroque violins and genuine harpsichords (rejecting Landowska's and Kirkpatrick's inauthentic, steel-framed, multi-pedalled monsters) – and to revive adequate playing skills, even virtuosity. These advances were sometimes accompanied by an uncompromising, often mindless, 'instrument fetishism' and zeal for 'authenticity', decreeing, for example, that 'Bach and the modern grand pianoforte are by logical definition, incompatible.' That was said in 1958 when Glenn Gould (who did not visit the Wigmore) and Rosalyn Tureck (who very much did) were at the height of their powers; yet puritanism seriously influenced current repertoire. By 1970 Misha Donat was reporting in the *Listener* that 'many great pianists are actually deterred by public opinion from playing Bach.'

Wigmore Hall programmes passively reflected these fashions and trends, along with continuing lurches between mediocrity and distinction. In February 1970 Joan Chissell noticed the 'perceptive musicianship' of a youthful Lindsay Quartet, while in December her *Times* colleague was still troubled by a spate of 'more inopportune debuts' including 'a spotlessly mediocre oboist', a 'rambling pianist' an 'attractive soprano' with a 'too ambitious repertoire', another pianist's 'almost chaotic struggle with Chopin's op. 35 Sonata', and yet another with 'brittle tone.' Soon the *Telegraph* was impressed by a 'young harpsichordist Trevor Pinnock' who played Bach and Rameau 'with the authority of an intellectually mature artist.' Only a minority of debuts have ever been distinguished, but venues, like people, are judged by the company they keep. Could the Hall ever be trusted to set minimum standards and, if not, how were people expected to be loyal, or at least select worthwhile concerts? Stephen Walsh warned against the common practice of 'testimonial' posters announcing 'indescribable brilliance', while agreeing that in the case of Maurice Hasson's violin playing 'all turned out to be true.' Recordings, much advertised and reviewed in 'best buy' fashion, had become effective flagbearers, so that in March 1971 'a crowded house' greeted the Fine Arts Quartet's already familiar Bartók (in every sense a sign of the times). And good newspapers, often employing authoritative critics, were still giving space and support (to today's readers another glimpse of sadly past times). In November *The Times* reported 'a big interested audience' recruited in November for 'someone whose development should be watched', Mitsuko Uchida. Did any of them return to hear a six-year-old whose Bach Partita and Mozart Sonata were 'naive, unrecognizable, but not unmusical'? Some events were easily identified; negatively in November 1972 when 'an audience of less than 20 saw a performer blowing bubbles for Stockhausen "Plus-minus" . . . 'a tedious musical joke,' concluded *The Times* – or positively in October 1973 when Youra Guller celebrated her Wigmore golden jubilee. 'A large audience with a gratifying number of London's pianistic élite present awarded a rousing ovation' after Thibaud's 'goddess of music' had tackled Beethoven op. 110 and the Liszt Sonata. So continued the arbitrary switchback of programmes.

§ *A unique place: an aura of significance.* The 75th birthday concerts in 1976 were an opportunity for celebration and fresh appraisal. Anniversary concerts, including Rubinstein, Pears, Bream, Perahia, Szeryng and, a superb culmination, Schwarzkopf, could stand comparison with the Bechstein inaugural, and provided an opportunity for some frank reassessment. After the South Bank acoustic, said Schwarzkopf in the *Guardian*, 'where I can't hear my own voice', the Wigmore was a 'totally different experience and the voice was rejuvenated.' Dominic Gill in the *Financial Times* similarly announced what was widely understood but rarely stated: 'Established artists as well as newcomers . . . find in Wigmore Street an attractive refuge from the wood and concrete acoustic of the South Bank.' The *Musical Times* also enthused, but touched upon some hard truths of economics: 'Steeped in character, attractively intimate, acoustically benevolent, Wigmore Hall is one of the most congenial places for music in London. Financial considerations have made it unfeasible for famous artists to appear regularly in the hall any more.' Even the weekly *New Society*, enjoying a short-lived prominence, was moved to pronounce momentarily upon high culture: if the South Bank had 'dimmed its glory' the Wigmore was still an important 'show case for promising young players' who could 'hire the Purcell Room for a night . . . but would the critics and public turn up? Wigmore Hall, with its traditions and genteel niceness, makes an ideal venue. You can ask your great-aunt along and she'll be at home.' Similar condescension from an equally unlikely source had been voiced in 1973 when the *Melody Maker* after a rare visit to cover a banjo and guitar concert, decided that the Wigmore was 'an unusual place, looking more like a luxurious (*sic*) funeral parlour than a concert auditorium.' All told, whatever people thought about its creature comforts in times of affluence, and despite constraints of size, the Hall survived as a potentially ideal place for music. Could the ideal be made practical?

William Lyne took over in 1966, but revolutions take time to accomplish, and it was not until the 1980s that his work bore ample fruit. Shifting the role of management from passive landlord to active fund-raiser, concert-promoter and audience-builder, he created a tradition of continuous artistic direction without precedent in Wigmore history. That story is told elsewhere, by Lyne himself and other contributors, and by the massive evidence of memorable concerts. Two which are especially pleasurable to recall were given by András Schiff on 13 and 16 November

*W*IGMORE
HALL

Friday 22 November 1996 at 7.30 pm

A Surprise Concert to Celebrate William Lyne's 30th Anniversary as Director of Wigmore Hall

We are grateful for the generous support of the Friends of Wigmore Hall for making this evening possible.

"Pass in, pass in," the angels say,
"In to the upper doors,
Nor count compartments of the floors,
But mount to paradise
By the stairway of surprise."

Ralph Waldo Emerson, Merlin

Wigmore Hall Director: William Lyne MBE, Hon. FTCL
Lessees: City of Westminster
The Wigmore Hall Trust
Registered Charity No. 1024838

Programme to commemorate William Lyne's 30th Anniversary as Director

1985, each devoted to one book of the '48'. Justly reviewed by Stephen Johnson in the *Musical Times* as 'an almost miraculous synthesis between intense expression and pure form', they confirmed two victories: for Bach on the piano, and for a completeness which even Busoni would never have contemplated. Nor could Bechstein Hall have found more than a handful of internationally recognised British artists. By the 1990s they were so prodigal as to invite alphabetical listing: Thomas Allen, the Arditti Quartet, Ian Bostridge, Julian Bream, Imogen Cooper, Barry Douglas, Endellion Quartet, the Florestan Trio, and so on. Lyne provided a consistent platform for such native talent, and for its best contemporaries from all over the world, steadily building the Hall's reputation for identifying and promoting excellence. But to appreciate the full scale of his achievement we must also remind ourselves of the environment against which it was accomplished.

It was during the 1980s, of course, that CDs completed the process by which technology took command of music, and by the nineties 'canned' sounds of all kinds became practically inescapable. The threat to cheapen even the best music, removing its roots and sense of occasion, had been forecast by Benjamin Britten in his masterly Aspen Lecture. Now the flood began to destroy long-established concepts of a finite repertoire which people could assimilate, along with related ideas of genre and, not least, canon (the exemplary works). In the early days of CD, concert promoters may have gained from its opening up of musical experience, but as the catalogues proliferated and digital sound became the norm, the threat to *live* music grew more menacing. How could audiences be persuaded to pay and make a special effort for what was seemingly available, comfortable, even free, at home. For society at large music was no longer rare and precious, perhaps no longer particularly desirable, often peripheral, as alternative pleasures became paramount. And in London the cost and inconvenience of concert-going was aggravated by miserably inadequate transport. In such conditions, in the sprawling metropolis of a market economy, where loyal audiences have always to be 'targeted' and persuaded to return, a reputable hall which puts music before all else becomes crucial for the very *survival* of concert life. Our argument has come full circle, beginning with the Bechstein Hall's approach to audiences through a distinctive *image*, but now subtly different. For today those hard-earned qualities of association which give distinction to a venue have acquired a wholly new meaning and significance. When 'mechanical' reproduction takes command of the arts, as Walter Benjamin famously argued, the living art can still retain an *aura* which sets it apart from a reproduction. In music that aura provides a lingering *raison d'être* for *live* performance, against all doubts about cost and convenience. Where better does the aura of music survive than in Wigmore Hall?

ANDRÁS SCHIFF

Designing Concert Programmes

Performing musicians who cannot or do not compose are re-creative artists. Their function is nevertheless vitally important, the voice of the composer speaks through the medium of the interpreter. Can performers be creative?

Yes, and the planning and construction of programmes is a real challenge of creativity. The following observations are based on the experiences of piano recitals and chamber music but they can equally be applied to other forms of music making.

Symphony orchestras all over the world are facing problems of declining audience attendance and part of the secret must be hidden in the art of programming. It's hardly surprising if audiences have become bored and tired by the constantly repeated recipe of overture-instrumental concerto-interval-symphony. With the advance of period instruments baroque and classical composers are mostly performed by their ensembles whereas specialist groups are frequently in charge of the presentation of contemporary music. The symphony orchestra is left with the repertory between these two poles from Beethoven to Shostakovich. Orchestras urgently need to explore new and old territories, invent novel forms of communication, if they want to avoid the sad destiny of dinosaurs.

But let's rather examine the case of the piano recital. The piano continues to be the most beloved instrument whose advantages outshine its limitations. It's not surprising that many of the greatest composers from Bach to Bartók were formidable keyboard players and wrote a major part of their entire output for these mechanisms. The piano's greatest glory is unquestionably its repertoire which is – justifiably – the envy of the other instruments. Are pianists aware of their treasures? Is this heritage well represented and taken care of?

A recital programme is the pianist's visiting card. It reflects on the performer's taste and intelligence in a way that the public is influenced by it

András Schiff with Peter Schreier

before she or he has played a single note. Unfortunately many players don't give adequate attention to this and the result is not only mediocrity but a certain uniformity of choice. It's enough to glance through the monthly diary of the world's concert halls. Endless rows of recitals with 'mixed salad' programmes: a little bit of Scarlatti, Bach or a harmless Haydn sonata to start with, followed by a meatier Beethoven, some Chopin to dream, followed by a wash of Debussy and a flash of Lisztian fireworks to make an impression and bring the house down. There can be no doubt that this recipe is effective (just as the orchestral scheme of overture-concerto-symphony is) but it's predictable and it's directed towards an audience whose only aim is to be entertained. The individual works on the programme are excellent but there is no thematic or musical connection between them, the pianist is merely presenting what she or he has learned for the occasion, according to the conventions and expectations of the public. In the Golden Age of piano playing this was more or less the norm. Listeners – and viewers – came to see and hear their favourite artists and it didn't matter what they played. Many of these virtuosos were alchemists who could turn dust into gold and enchant everybody with their magical witchcraft. While we continue to admire these artists through their recordings with awe, reverence and nostalgia it cannot be denied that the general taste for piano recitals has changed considerably. This is largely due to particular musicians, first and foremost to Artur Schnabel. This wonderful musician and pianist (also a serious composer) believed that life was too short to play anything but the very best music. Only music that is infinitely better than it can ever be played. His programmes were notable for their seriousness, where 'the second half is just as boring as the first half'. Schnabel did wonders with Mozart, Beethoven, Schumann and Brahms and he virtually rediscovered the Schubert sonatas. He had also educated a public that became more demanding. They came to hear Beethoven and Schubert, played by Schnabel, not the other way round.

Today's often lamentable musical life can claim that Mozart's concertos are regularly played (not only K466 and 491) and that Schubert's sonatas are as much appreciated as Beethoven's. This is a real cause for joy and no doubt that Schnabel is smiling behind his cigar in Heaven.

In the visual arts it's quite usual that we go to see exhibitions dedicated to a single artist's work. It's instructive and educational to observe the development, evolution and inter-connections in a particular *oeuvre*. A similar experience awaits us in concerts that are designed mono-thematically, based on one single composer. Not all composers are equally suited to this treatment. The obvious ones are Bach, Haydn, Mozart, Beethoven, Schubert and Schumann. Their keyboard music is so incredibly rich, complex, and of such variety in form and expression that we can never get overfilled by them. These masters deserve our utmost attention so that the single concert can be extended into a series or cycle of events. Bach's

Artur Schnabel

Well-Tempered Clavier, Beethoven's 32 sonatas and Schubert's sonatas are beautifully enjoyable in parts; in their entirety they are mightily impressive. Mozart's piano sonatas – with some exceptions – are not among his highest achievements like those sonatas for piano and violin or his incomparable piano concertos. Nevertheless they are well worth hearing in a cycle especially when we add to them some shorter works like A minor Rondo, the B minor Adagio, the little Gigue, and some of the Variation sets. Haydn's sonatas are also not all on the same level but there are about two dozen absolute masterpieces among them. Many of these are infrequently played and therefore the systematic presentation of Haydn's sonatas and shorter pieces (Capriccio, Fantasie, Variations F minor) could be an almost missionary task. Schumann is a magical composer, a great poet whose output for the piano is prodigious. His first twenty-three opus numbers are all written for his favourite instrument and through Clara's art and inspiration we can follow this invisible line until the tragic end of his life, testified by *Gesänge der Frühe* and the Variations in E flat major (*Geistervariationen*). It's not necessary to play his complete works in concert but an intelligent selection can be arranged into three or four programmes alternating the well-known pieces (*Carnaval, Fantasie,*

Kreisleriana) with the lesser-known (*Humoreske, Noveletten, Concert sans Orchestre*) and the virtually unknown late works. It's a pity that most pianists are content to concentrate on a handful of Schumann's compositions because these are the ones that everybody knows and plays. Curiosity should urge them to read through all the other volumes and discover hidden treasures.

Haydn's and Schumann's genius can be even better served if we combine the piano music with the chamber music. Haydn's phenomenal piano trios and songs, Schumann's Lieder, trios, quartet and quintet offer the most attractive alternations.

Domenico Scarlatti, Debussy and Bartók are among my most beloved composers. However – and this is not a criticism – their music is not well served by monothematic planning. Their works do not have the variety of scale and form that distinguishes the former group of masters. Programming too many short pieces is a mistake, the audience's attention cannot be sustained. Therefore it's best to devote half of the concert to these, completing it with another composer of similar or contrasting nature.

Scarlatti is the Chopin of the eighteenth century (more of the great Pole later). His life was one of the most interesting ones and his 550-odd sonatas are real marvels. This Neapolitan genius under the influence of the Iberian Peninsula has created little wonders, all in binary form, yet so very different from each other. Pianists who play two or three of these as an introduction to their recital – usually the same ones that they know through recordings by Lipatti, Horowitz and Michelangeli – can barely pay lip-service to Scarlatti. At least half a concert – twelve to fourteen sonatas – is needed to appreciate the full range of the music. Most of these were conceived in pairs and the performer should respect this (it's also not advisable to separate a Bach prelude from the following fugue). The sequence must be chosen with great care leaving room for contrasts of expression and following a certain pattern of tonality. One can move in a circle of fifths: C major – G major – D major, etc., or even better in thirds: C major – E minor – G major, etc., but one should avoid steps that are too shocking, like F minor after E major. We can begin or end the concert with Scarlatti and in the remaining part play something big and substantial like a Schumann sonata.

Debussy vignettes and water-colours can be best appreciated in the proximity of Bach, Mozart and Chopin, his preferred composers. Debussy didn't like Beethoven and it's counter-productive to force them together.

Bartók's piano music – with the exception of the 1926 Sonata – consists of shorter pieces. He was a phenomenal pianist and his own works reflect the influences of earlier masters. Even among the greatest composers Bartók's spirit shines like a diamond, therefore it's best to combine him with Bach or Beethoven. Haydn is also an excellent partner for him because of his crystalline form, his humour and sense of folklore.

Frederic Chopin is one of the greatest masters of the piano and furthermore a divine musician who happens to have expressed himself through his instrument. There hadn't been any shortage of countless all-Chopin recitals by specialists and 'Chopinhauers'. Few composers are played so frequently, so badly. And again it is most questionable if a whole evening spent with Chopin only is a good idea. Apart from the Sonatas and the Ballades, the Barcarolle and the F minor Fantasie, maybe a few of the Polonaises, most of his pieces are perfect miniatures. Chopin was a marvellous performer who disliked public concerts; during his life he only appeared between thirty and forty times in public. His Preludes, Nocturnes and Mazurkas are intimately private confessions. It's probably better to let him share the programme with others and we should keep in mind that he didn't like any of his contemporaries and even of Beethoven he only performed one sonata, the one with another funeral march (op. 26). Chopin adored Bach and Mozart and they provide the best company to him together with the mercurial Scarlatti with whom he seems to have a close affinity.

Listening to a lot of Brahms reminds me of the Tintorettos at the Scuola di San Rocco in Venice (John Ruskin must disagree). All this magnificent splendour that is so dark, heavy and ponderous it makes one want to go out to the fresh air and breathe freely. Brahms's music is not like that – it's certainly not served well by heavy-handed performances lacking in clarity and transparency. After having done the complete chamber music in five programmes (fifteen wonderful works) I feel that a whole evening of Brahms is too much to digest. It needs to be balanced by something lighter, airier, to achieve the contrast of chiaroscuro, light and shade. This leads us to varied recital programmes that aren't necessarily mixed salads. Masterpieces by Handel, Mendelssohn, Smetana, Janáček, Reger and others have to be introduced in an imaginative manner. There can be musical, historical, geographical or national connections between them. Consider the following:

Bach: Chromatic Fantasy and Fugue
Reger: Variations and Fugue on a theme by Bach
Handel: Suite in B flat major
Brahms: Variations and Fugue on a theme by Handel

Brahms's theme is the same as the Handel Suite's variation theme. Everything relates to everything else. Or how about this one:

Scarlatti: 13 Sonatas
Interval
Janáček: Sonata 1905
Smetana: 3 Polkas op. 8
Chopin: 5 Mazurkas
Bartók: Sonata 1926

The two halves form a huge contrast not only historically but temperamentally. First we inhale the air and light of the Mediterranean followed by four composers connected by their Eastern European origin and their quest for nationalism and patriotism. N.B. This *list* only contains composers that are very dear to me (hence the obvious absence of *Liszt*). Others may feel equally attracted to different ones, and there is nothing wrong with that provided that they give ample thought to programming. The piano repertoire is enormous and nobody can play everything equally well. It's essential to be self-critical and to choose only those works that we love and that we feel emotionally, intellectually, temperamentally close to.

We must talk about the inclusion of new music. Every musician must have a keen interest in the latest creations but putting these into the programme must be suggested by enthusiasm and devotion, not just a sense of duty. New compositions are often premièred at contemporary music festivals and many of them never get a second hearing. It's useful to take the best pieces out of this neo-snobbish ghetto, and put them together with the best of the past. The real test for the modern composer is to see how well he or she can stand next to Mozart.

The beginning of the concert is all-important. The first note must

Annie Fischer

carry the full responsibility of the performer. Therefore it's essential what we start the programme with. The audience is not quite ready, there are latecomers, people talking and fidgeting. We must open with something that will immediately command attention. This can be achieved by sudden exclamation or delicate whispering. The first piece on the programme doesn't have to be long, it's actually quite wrong to play the most substantial piece at the beginning because it upsets the balance of the two halves. Pianists who open a recital with Beethoven's op. 111 or Schubert's last sonata are not aware of the weight of these works. The unforgettable Annie Fischer told me about one of them, 'He hasn't got a soul.' Thomas Mann's Doktor Faustus explains why there can be nothing more said after the Arietta of op. 111. Not even another piece by Beethoven, let alone Liszt or Rachmaninov. Is it possible that certain pianists haven't read Thomas Mann?

There is one creative art form that is similar to programming and that is – don't laugh – cooking. Not the actual preparation of a dish but the arrangement, composition and balancing of a meal require similar attention. A well-balanced meal – starter, soup, main course, vegetables and dessert alongside which delicious wines are served – will raise the spirit and not cause indigestion. A meal consisting of tiny little snacks is as unsatisfactory as a piano recital of small encore pieces. Real satisfaction can only be achieved if the menu is carefully designed, with an introduction slowly building up towards the culmination and still leaving space for a few final delicacies. Music is food for the heart, the brain, the whole organism.

'If music be the food of love, play on.'

Robert Cowan

Pianists at the Wigmore Hall

If Harley Street is a Mecca for medical practice and Bond Street a long-standing promoter of fashion, nearby Wigmore Street has to be one of the principal witnesses to London's musical past. It was there, in the Hall now known as the 'Wigmore' but that was once the 'Bechstein', that pianists ranging from Busoni in the 1900s to Brendel in the 1990s disseminated great music among dedicated audiences.

Sifting through past Wigmore programmes makes one all but weep at the late arrival of recording technology. What wouldn't we have paid to hear Busoni play Beethoven's great E flat Sonata op. 109 at the Hall's inaugural concert in May 1901? Not that upcoming technology was entirely lost on the Wigmore's management. In March 1927 there was a 'musical evening with the new scientific gramophone, the "vivational" Columbia and new electrical recordings.' Many of the artists programmed – they included Ignaz Friedman, Felix Weingartner and William Murdoch – had performed in the Hall live, so this new-fangled 'miracle' must have seemed doubly bizarre. But before cherry-picking some of the more extraordinary programmes in the Hall's astonishing history, let me call on the memories of two grand ladies who played there. World-renowned Chicago-born Bach specialist Rosalyn Tureck is now 86 but was once a firebrand virtuoso who toyed with the most radical of new musics. 'I made my English debut at the Wigmore Hall in 1953 with a series of three weekly Bach recitals,' she told me recently. 'I played Preludes and Fugues, Suites and the *Goldberg Variations*. When it came to the third recital, I arrived at the Hall through the back stage entrance. Emmie Tillett, who was my manager at the time, was there to greet me. "Isn't this exciting?" she said. But as I didn't know what she was referring to, I simply gave her a smile and let it go at that. So she left, and I went out and played my recital. What I *didn't* know beforehand was that additional seats had been placed on the stage, something that had apparently only happened

Rosalyn Tureck

on one previous occasion in the Hall's history – and that was for a Kathleen Ferrier recital.' Tureck recalls the cause of Tillett's 'excitement' as being 'a mad rush of people trying to get into the Hall. Police had to stop the traffic from one end of the block to the other.'

Adoring receptions are, one has to say, comparatively rare; but Tureck's response to the Hall itself rings a familiar tune. 'It's a beautiful hall, very intimate,' she recalls fondly. 'The sound never becomes distorted because of "flaws in the materials". It has a wonderful back stage room. And I can tell you that any artist will be grateful for a harmonious, spacious area, something that many contemporary halls do not have: they're so ugly and square that it's a comparative hardship to be in them. Not so the Wigmore, where there's an artistic – no, an *aesthetic* – atmosphere. I'm talking about a quality of closeness, of communication that's of course very significant and means a great deal to me. I suppose it's like the two sides of one coin: a harmonious "back stage" where one can communicate with

Mark Hambourg

oneself, and then this intimacy on stage where you communicate with the audience.'

London-based Michal Hambourg is Tureck's junior by a mere five years. Michal is the daughter of the celebrated piano virtuoso Mark Hambourg, a favoured pupil of the great Polish pianist, teacher and composer Theodor Leschetizky whose colourful playing style courted both admiration and outrage. Mark Hambourg gave at least one all-Chopin Wigmore recital, that was in October 1922, just one month after Alexander Siloti had been playing Bach and Liszt. Indeed, father and daughter both appeared at the Hall. 'Everybody liked the venue,' says Michal. 'It had an aura of homeliness: it was very "red plush" and a little dowdy, what the Germans call *gemüt-lich*, sympathetic.' As to the audience, it was usually 'English musical establishment', as she puts it. 'I remember hearing Harriet Cohen play a group of pieces by Arnold Bax. I also remember that Bax came onto the stage afterwards in the most deplorable suit.'

Some of the most mouth-watering slices of Wigmore history occurred earlier on in the century. 1902 saw the appearance of Venezuelan-born Teresa Carreño, a pianist whose personal appearance earned her the nickname 'Valkyrie of the Piano'. Carreño's legendary power would have been usefully employed in Chopin's B minor Sonata and Schumann's *Fantasie*, not to mention Beethoven's Sonata op. 109. That was in mid-February, whereas two weeks later the English Clara Schumann-pupil Fanny Davies was playing Fauré, Ferrari and Sgambati. Another English pupil of Clara Schumann was Adelina de Lara who, in April 1907, performed Brahms's F minor Piano Quartet with the Kruse Quartet.

Australian composer-pianist Percy Grainger crops up on numerous occasions, and so does the celebrated teacher Tobias Matthay, whose wife regularly gave recitations. Matthay's star pupil Myra Hess made her debut in 1907 but in October 1904 Hess's contemporary Irene Scharrer was scheduled to give 'her first piano recital – on Thursday afternoon, 27 October'.

Michal Hambourg recalls her father's opinion of composer-pianist Eugen d'Albert: 'He was frightfully temperamental and a perfect beast but had a most marvellous sense of rhythm.' D'Albert gave two recitals in April 1904, the first consisting entirely of works by Beethoven (Sonatas opp. 31/2, 51/2, 57, 53 and the C minor Variations), the second of Chopin's *Fantasie* and Third Sonata, and Liszt's B minor Sonata.

Still, the Hall's programmes didn't always go according to plan. An early recital that Leschetizky pupil Benno Moiseiwitsch gave in November 1913 was hampered by – and here I quote the programme – 'the lateness of receipt of Mr. John Powell's *Sonata Teutonica*.' The note continued: 'It is impossible to include the work in the present programme, but Mr. Moiseiwitsch will play it in his recital in February next.' In the event, he played it in March – but at least the promise was kept.

Benno Moiseiwitsch

Michal recalls being taken to hear Moiseiwitsch. 'He was a great friend of our family whom I used to hear playing and practising a lot at our home. He gave two Schumann recitals at the Wigmore, and to witness him perform the *Fantasie* – which was the first piece of music I can remember hearing – was a pivotal experience for me. I heard him play it twice. In the second performance, he lost his way in the first movement, which is what happens to people when they're very, very nervous. When you start the first movement you have to make up your mind whether it's going to be an affair of the heart or an accurate recollection of the notes. My father said, "I want you to hear this, because if he really takes off, it'll be quite unforgettable." Well he did – and it was!'

It was during the early 1900s that another Leschetizky pupil, the English pianist Frank Merrick, played a programme that featured Bach-d'Albert and Beethoven's Sonata op. 111 as well as a smaller group that included works by Leschetizky and the pianist himself. A year earlier, the *Sunday Times* had observed that in Bach, Beethoven and Chopin, Merrick 'showed a mental comprehensiveness and brilliancy of execution that excited the liveliest applause.'

Pianist-composer York Bowen appeared in 1905 playing J. B. McEwen's Sonata in B minor, the D minor Sonata by B. J. Dale and Glazunov's Sonata in B flat. In Bowen's case, it was a 1904 edition of the *Daily Telegraph* that had observed how 'he phrases as only a pianist who is also an artist can.' In 1924, Bowen was back at the Wigmore playing his own F minor Sonata (which had been published during the previous year). No other pianist of the period was more closely associated with Beethoven's music than the Scottish-born Liszt pupil Frederic Lamond. In 1904, *The Times* wrote that 'it seems to us that this pianist shows at each visit a greater emotional power than before', and it was in May 1903 that Lamond gave a hugely demanding series of Beethoven sonata recitals. To give just an example of his gargantuan programming, on 24 April, not content with offering the 50-minute *Hammerklavier* Sonata (which, incidentally, Busoni would perform in 1906), he also played opp. 110 and 111, the *Waldstein* and the *Appassionata*.

In November 1936 Lamond marked the 50th Anniversary of his first London appearance with a series of five recitals. The first consisted of Schumann's *Fantasie*, *Carnaval* and *Symphonic Studies*; the second, was given over entirely to Chopin (including the B minor Sonata); the third featured Brahms's F minor Sonata and *Paganini Variations* (with Reger's *Beethoven Variations* thrown in for good measure); the fourth was all Liszt (including the B minor Sonata) and the fifth, all Beethoven (sonatas).

American-Polish Leopold Godowsky was known both as a pianist and a composer and his early 1902 programmes are truly mouth-watering. One featured the *Appassionata*, Liszt's *Scherzo and March* and some Wagner arranged by Joseph Rubinstein, and the other had Schumann's *Fantasie* and Brahms's *Paganini Variations* as its musical centrepieces. It was reported that at the concert (or one that was fairly close to it) the great Ukrainian Chopin pianist Vladimir de Pachmann 'waved his hands with delight'. Even more fascinating is the discovery that in May 1903 Godowsky performed Franck and Brahms sonatas with the celebrated French violinist Jacques Thibaud.

Leopold Godowsky   *Jacques Thibaud*

Pachmann himself was always something of a 'draw'. In May 1903 he programmed Schumann's G minor Sonata, Bach and Chopin, giving an all-Chopin recital (including the B minor Sonata) a month or so later. Liszt's last surviving pupil was the Portuguese pianist José Vianna da Motta, an astonishing player whose Wigmore appearances in 1903 included Weber (Sonata op. 39) and major Beethoven (opp. 26, 57, 106 & 111). Liszt pupil Emil Sauer (in the early 1920s the 'von' was not obligatory) played the *Appassionata* in January 1924, a week before Solomon also performed it (the Wigmore programme sequences are full of fascinating repertoire duplications). Regarding von Sauer Michal recalls that 'he was a wonderful apparition. He dressed the way Liszt must have dressed, in a cloak with a red satin lining, aided by a walking stick with a silver top. His entourage consisted of three or four exquisite nubile young ladies.'

Not all the names that appear in those early programmes were poised on the edge of distinction. Solomon, for one, had wowed audiences long before the First World War but in 1917 (the year in which the Bechstein Hall became the Wigmore) he gave a 'farewell recital'. He was just fifteen at the time but had sagely decided to 'retire from the concert platform for a considerable time in order to devote himself to study and the acquisition of a still more extensive repertoire.' He was later to become one of the Wigmore's best-loved stars.

Concert Direction E. A. MICHELL

WIGMORE HALL Wigmore Street, W.

Tuesday, June 5th, at 3.15

Photo by Dover Street Studio

SOLOMON

Farewell Recital

Saint-Saëns played in 1906 and Arthur Rubinstein – whose appearances in the 1930s were to draw great critical acclaim – gave two recitals as early as 1912. Artur Schnabel first appeared at the Wigmore early in 1904, fresh from his Queen's Hall triumph in Brahms's Second Piano Concerto under Hans Richter. The notices had been more appreciative than perceptive. 'His touch is crisp and at times a little hard,' wrote a critic from the *Sunday Times*, 'and his accuracy is quite remarkable.' That

Arthur Rubinstein

would certainly change, though the 'wonderful command of the keyboard' that the *Morning Post* had noted was a persistent attribute. What was especially interesting about those early Schnabel programmes was the adventurous choice of repertoire: Schubert's posthumous A major Sonata (who else played it in those days?), a Schumann group and two relatively unfamiliar Beethoven sonatas (opp. 78 and 79).

Michal Hambourg recalls how Schnabel, the Polish-American pianist Josef Hofmann and her father were the 'three Leschetizky prodigies together', who lived in the same boarding house. It also seems that they were three 'men behaving badly'. 'All three were expelled for putting a bust of

Beethoven in the landlady's bed at night,' said Michal. 'She went to the Professor and said that she simply couldn't keep them!' Leschetizky would regularly take all three lads to see the gypsies because 'it was they who had the best understanding of the rhythm of music . . . and to hear them was essential if you wanted to play Liszt's *Hungarian Rhapsodies* properly.' In 1924, Hofmann played a recital that included Beethoven's Sonata op. 111, as well as music by Gluck, Saint-Saëns and some of his own work.

One of Michal Hambourg's most enduring memories was of the Ukrainian pianist-composer Moritz Rosenthal. As she herself recalls: 'It was a policy of my father's to take me to hear recitals by those of his friends who were also great artists, so that I could understand certain styles of playing. I think the first master that I heard was Moritz Rosenthal. My father wanted me to understand the rhythm of the mazurka, and he said that Rosenthal was one of the greatest exponents of it. I can remember the hall being absolutely crammed with people, when on came this rather plump, foursquare but strangely elegant person with the most wonderful moustache. It was quite a preoccupation for someone of my age, seeing a moustache like that. I'd never seen anything of that sort before – and he had such very small feet.' Michal remembers going home to learn a Mazurka in G, 'being stopped by my Dad who urged me to remember how Rosenthal had played.'

Michal might have been remembering one of the seven 'Historical Concerts of music from Bach to Brahms' that Rosenthal gave at the Wigmore during April and May in 1936. The first recital featured Bach's *Chromatic Fantasia and Fugue*, as well as music by Scarlatti, Couperin, Daquin and Handel. In the second, Rosenthal played Beethoven's Sonatas opp. 57, 109 and 111 plus the C minor Variations, while in the third he offered Beethoven's *Pathétique*, Weber's Sonata op. 39 and Schubert's *Wanderer Fantasie*. The fourth recital was devoted entirely to Schumann (*Kreisleriana* and the *Fantasie*), the fifth to Chopin (including the B minor Sonata), the sixth to the likes of Field, Moscheles, Henselt, Thalberg, 'Chopin arr Liszt' and Liszt's own B minor Ballade (what a recital that must have been!). The final recital in the series was given over to works by Anton Rubinstein, Mendelssohn and Brahms (his *Variations on a Hungarian Song*). And don't forget that in Rosenthal's heyday, Brahms was 'new music'. But perhaps the most exciting discovery (at least for this enthusiast) was a recital that Alexander Scriabin gave at 3 pm on the afternoon of 20 March 1914 – just a year before his untimely death at the age of 43. Earlier in the month Scriabin had appeared at the Queen's Hall playing his Piano Concerto and the piano part in his recently composed orchestral tone poem (or 'Fifth Symphony') *Prometheus*. The *Observer* of 1 March had claimed that Scriabin 'might well be considered the apostolic successor of Chopin'. The notice continued: 'By a process of evolution distinctly visible in any intimate study of his works as they rapidly succeeded and superseded each other, he has attained a technique that permits of musical utterances in which no suggestion can be found of the tradition on which they were based.' Quite so, and anyone who attended that Bechstein recital (where he played music from opp. 3, 8, 11, 32 and 59 plus the Third Sonata) would probably have agreed.

Mark and Michal Hambourg played Busoni's *Indian Fantasy* but the most prominent Busoni specialist of the day (aside from the composer himself) was the German-Dutch pianist Egon Petri who, as a relatively young man (he was still in his early thirties at the time) performed the six Elegies. The date was 30 March 1914, whereas in June of the same year the celebrated Polish Chopin player Raoul Koczalski was performing Korngold's op. 6 and Max Reger's op. 84.

The roll-call of Wigmore pianists is as endless as it is fascinating, far too long in fact to chronicle in anything less than a very substantial list – or a very thick book. I'll close by quoting a few highlights that took my own fancy. One was a recital that the distinguished French pianist Robert Casadesus gave in April 1927, just a few days after his twenty-eighth birthday. The programme had included Liszt's B minor Sonata. 'His playing is quite beyond reproach,' reported *The Times* of an earlier recital, while *The Morning Post* celebrated 'a musician of quite exceptional insight, yet conscientious enough to practise self-effacement.'

Fanny Davies and the German clarinettist Richard Mühlfeld played the Brahms clarinet sonatas (which were written expressly for Mühlfeld), in 1905 and in 1907 there was a whole concert devoted to Felix Weingartner's compositions (with the composer himself participating).

Polish virtuoso Ignaz Friedman appeared in 1924 in repertoire that included the Bach-Busoni *Chaconne*, Schumann's *Carnaval* and Chopin's

B minor Sonata. Wilhelm Kempff gave two recitals during the same year where he played his op. 12 *Fantasias* and – get this! – his own custom-built arrangement of the Scherzo from Bruckner's Eighth Symphony. It was also in 1924 that Alfred Cortot programmed Mussorgsky's *Pictures at an Exhibition*; but you would have waited a further thirteen years to hear Joseph Lhévinne play Beethoven's *Waldstein* Sonata.

The noted Australian pianist Noel Mewton-Wood played Schubert, Schumann, Medtner and Debussy in 1943 and in 1944 Frank Merrick gave the first English performance of Prokofiev's Seventh Sonata (that was on 22 February). The writer on music Peter Stadlen showed his mettle in two Spring 1944 recitals, where he played Beethoven's *Hammerklavier* and *Diabelli Variations*. Rudolf Serkin had offered us his *Hammerklavier* twelve years earlier (in 1930 he could also be heard in duet with his violinist father-in-law Adolf Busch) and in the same year (1932) young 'Ruda' Firkušný played Schumann's *Fantasie*, Bach-Busoni, Schubert-Liszt, Smetana and Novák.

And there are many others: Antheil, Arrau, Babin, Backhaus, Bauer, Borovsky, Borwick, Brailowsky, Britten, Casals (yes, on piano), Chasins, Ciampi, Cole, Curzon, Dohnányi, Doniach, Elinson, Erdmann, Février, Fischer (both Annie and Edwin), Gieseking, Harty, Hope, Horsley, Horszowski, Julius Isserlis, Katchen, Kitchin, Kraus, Lipatti, Lortat, Lympany, Meyer, Milkina, Ney, Niedzielski, Nikisch, Franz Osborn, Pauer, Pouishnoff, Prokofiev, Reizenstein, Landon Ronald, Rummel, Samuel, Sapelnikoff, Smeterlin, the Cyrils Scott and Smith, Szpinalski, Uninsky, Verne, Vronsky and Wührer. And that's just a smattering of names you might know, hugely gifted men and women who at least made a recording or two. There are many more names that you probably won't be familiar with, which begs the question: what of the countless 'second-tier' players whose musical gifts are also worthy of commemoration but who never made records? Perhaps when we pause to remember the Rubinsteins, the Kempffs and the Rosenthals we should also give a thought to those forgotten mortals whose efforts were as much a part of the Wigmore Hall's wonderful history as the masters who inspired them.

The Artists Speak

A young inexperienced singer will never realise it until much later in his or her life: the opportunity to perform at Wigmore Hall is one of the most blessed experiences of one's career. I've travelled all over the world as a singer, but nothing rivals the very special sound and atmosphere that is the Wigmore Hall. Cherish that first time, nurture it, and then pray that you may have many more such happy occasions in your life. To be surrounded by such excellence is what we should all be aiming for.

SIR THOMAS ALLEN

Wigmore Hall, write about it. I wish I could *sing* about it. Because singing is so easy in this gem of a hall. Standing on the stage one has the feeling that one sings through a mild type of speaking trumpet: the sound seems to be augmented when it is transported to the last seat at the back. Nothing can be more reassuring to a singer than this sensation. When I reached the time to relax and sit back in a chair in the Hall, I heard the sounds arrive, crystal clear, and synthesised, instead of analysed. Music making, music hearing, all is sheer pleasure in Wigmore Hall!

From the stage the Hall looks – even when the specs were left behind in the artist's room – harmonious and warmly receiving. The art nouveau decorations are famous; and indeed from my seat I could finally enjoy them completely.

The quality of a hall is also made by its audience. A singer's soul can sing, but when there is no echo there is just no concert. IT does not happen. The Wigmore Hall audience is a fascinating crowd for an artist: they concentratedly receive the music and react to it. Not only by applause but rather by intense silence, or at times by a good laugh. You Londoners may not be aware that you and Wigmore Hall together are unique in the world. You turn the pages as one man, and it was certainly *not* in Wigmore Hall that I had to ask: Do you mind when I sing while you cough?

Last but not least: the staff and its Director.

In the sixties already I sang here, and a gentleman of many years' service as a page turner gave me, unexperienced beginner, tremendous courage by his friendly remarks.

Later on, the unsurpassable Director William Lyne allowed us to sing a cabaret programme for a change.

When that evening was over I could use a refresher indeed. Who else than William put the vodka and orange juice in my room . . . and made it a tradition?!

Dearest Wigmore Hall, my heartfelt best wishes for your new century.

Elly Ameling

In 1983 I was allowed out of the GDR and behind the 'iron-curtain' for the first time, to travel to London for the Walther Gruner Song Competition. I won first prize in this competition and with it a Lieder recital at the Wigmore Hall. In November 1983 I was privileged to make my Wigmore Hall debut with no less an accompanist than Geoffrey Parsons. One can never again feel quite the elation of such a unique experience. It almost drove the nervousness away. And this is precisely one of the special qualities of this extraordinary auditorium: where young, still unknown artists constantly have the chance to gather their first experiences from a renowned concert stage. One feels at ease from first entry onwards – almost protected.

There are many reasons for this. First there's the lovely architecture and the superlative acoustic that goes with it.

And then there's the audience: the newcomer or 'established' artist alike can be sure of having a knowledgeable and critical audience out there – an audience before whom no artist can hide behind the term 'established'.

Such a discriminating audience is developed through familiarity with the music. And here the programmes to be heard at the Wigmore Hall achieve wonders. It is always adventure, pleasure and stimulus combined, to study the monthly programmes in all their diversity. (Sadly, for the practising musician, opportunities to attend concerts are far too rare . . .)

The world behind the stage which the public never sees is almost as important to the artist as the stage itself. Here also the Wigmore Hall is unique in the world, both in terms of spaciousness and above all for the warmth of the staff. A friendly word or encouraging look at the right moment just before going on can help such a lot.

However one should never overlook the tradition of this house. The photos in the foyer and entrance stairs speak their own language. In the presence of this tradition, it always fills me with pride to be allowed to make an appearance.

May the art of this platform, so steeped in tradition, continue to survive in this fast-living age. I'm sure that artists and audiences will thank us for it in a hundred years' time.

Olaf Bär

WIGMORE HALL CENTENARY 2001

How sweet the moonlight sleeps upon this bank! Here will we sit, and
let the sounds of music creep in our ears : soft stillness and the night
Become the touches of sweet harmony . Look how the floor of heaven
Is thick inlaid with patines of bright gold : There's not the smallest orb
that thou behold'st But in his motion like an angel sings Still quiring
to the young-eyed cherubins ; Such harmony is in immortal souls :
But whilst this muddy vesture of decay Doth grossly close it in , we
cannot hear it . Come, ho, and wake Diana with a hymn! With sweet-
est touches pierce your mistress' ear , And draw her home with music , I
am never merry when I hear sweet music . The reason is , your spirits
are attentive The man that hath no music in himself , Nor is not
moved with concord of sweet sounds , Is fit for treasons , stratagems and
spoils ; The motions of his spirit are dull as night , And his affections dark
as Erebus : Let no such man be trusted . Music! Hark! It is your
music of the house . Methinks it sounds much sweeter than by day .
Silence bestows that virtue on it . How many things by season season'd are .
To their right praise and true perfection Peace, ho! The moon sleeps
with Endymion , And would not be awaked , Stillness soft and the night
Become the touches of sweet harmony . William Shakespeare

Calligraphy by BARBARA BONNEY

Wigmore Hall will always have a special place in my heart – because that is where I began my international career with my first really important recital. I was lucky, because it has wonderful acoustics, it has warmth and charm and it inspires awe, because some of the world's greatest artists have stood on that stage and performed before an audience which is among the most knowledgeable in the world. Wigmore Hall is unique and may it always remain so.

CECILIA BARTOLI

I must have have come to Wigmore Hall first in the late 1970s, brought by friends to hear a piano recital by the late Terence Judd. A few years later, and I was coming regularly from school to hear Lieder recitals and the Songmakers' Almanac. Then university, and a long gap in my knowledge of the Hall until I started entering singing competitions, many of which took place at the Wigmore. I never did very well but after one, I had a wonderfully encouraging letter from William Lyne virtually promising a concert there when the time was ripe. It's one of the handful of reasons I became a singer.

Of course, wherever you go in the world to sing Lieder, Wigmore Hall is a name to conjure with, universally respected, a sort of brand name almost unique in classical music. For me, the greatest pleasure is the sense of having such a fantastic institution in my home city, a true artistic home, and one with such an atmosphere of warmth and support.

IAN BOSTRIDGE

London born, my own musical life has always revolved round the Wigmore Hall.

I was taken as a child – I particularly remember the nearly blind Rubinstein apologising from the stage at the end of the concert for missing some of the jumps in Chopin's B flat minor Scherzo – and some of the first concert tickets I actually bought for myself were for the ground-breaking Fauré series. I went to every one and the atmosphere and feeling of discovery in those concerts, the first of William Lyne's pioneering 'themed' series, has stayed with me ever since.

One of the principal reasons I set my heart on becoming a chamber pianist was coming along so often to the Wigmore and hearing Geoffrey Parsons play and Roger Vignoles, Graham Johnson, Irwin Gage, Ian Brown, Menahem Pressler . . . I never thought of their role as subsidiary or unequal – a tribute of course to their artistry and also to the Wigmore's stage, perfect for the intimacy and communion between musicians making chamber music. The pianists were the lucky ones, it seemed to me, because they got to play there so much more often than their partners.

My actual Wigmore Hall debut concert was on 31 January 1983 and it remains probably the most exciting and unforgettable concert of my life. Six of us altogether, every one of us playing at the Wigmore for the first time. We wanted our concert to be a tribute to a composer very close to all our hearts, Francis Poulenc, a special concert because 31 January was the 20th anniversary of his untimely death.

Of course we had no idea whether anyone but our close family and friends would come to hear such a programme; we also had to persuade William Lyne to let a bunch of relative unknowns take over the Hall for quite a controversial piece of programming.

Now I know him better I realise we needn't have worried – William's instinct for something worth doing will always win out over mundane practical considerations. And he was right, of course. Just before I walked out on stage the concert organiser came into the Green Room to tell me about 100 people had been turned away. I was astonished: Why? – I asked. Because, she explained, the house was completely sold out and no seats could be found for them.

As I walked out on to the Wigmore Hall stage for the first time I knew straight away that concert halls didn't come better than this – that this was my musical home.

JULIUS DRAKE

Highly polished brass door handles – yes, that was my first impression. And dear William . . . sweet William . . . shy William, untypically extending his hand in welcome. At least the Germans only shake hands on each and every occasion. He has to kiss the Russians!

My agent had crammed in a Liederabend between two performances at Covent Garden. I felt under pressure and was grumpy . . . Poor William!

Gently, he led me to the Green Room, and onto the podium, and the Hall began to work its magic. The glorious acoustic, a perfect size for Lieder.

Would I like something to drink?

'No, thank you, perhaps later.'

'And after the recital?'

'Well – a cold beer never tastes better – or even a slightly warm English one.' (No, no, I'm a great Bitter fan.)

Once said, never forgotten. After every one of my recitals, ready and waiting in the Gerald Moore Room, a tray with a freshly poured glass of lager.

And then the recital itself and the surprise as I walked onto the platform, nervous as always, and felt that incredibly warm welcome from the public which was to remain such an important factor when nerves or indisposition made the opening of the concavely curved door, at shortly after 7.30 pm, something to dread.

And what a public they are. They know so much, and indeed they have heard so much, and so many. I hope they realise how important they have become in international terms (thanks to William Lyne's great programming). No compromises necessary at the Wigmore. No pick-of-the-pops from Purcell to Poulenc, with a Puccini parody as encore. My mission to sing 'literary' programmes, 'thematic' programmes, 'poetic' programmes – by definition 'difficult' programmes – was no problem for the Wigmore public. The more obscure, the more they seemed to lap it up. An *a cappella* Aribert Reimann cycle without a text translation in the programme was listened to with breathless concentration.

They like to laugh a lot too. We've all had great fun during the master classes of recent years. Long may this public keep fighting the cultural-eventing and cross-over crisis!

My visits became annual – and after my second or third visit, I was asked to provide a signed photograph. How proud I was whenever I walked into the Green Room to see my picture hanging there, until I realised that the photos are changed to coincide with the visit of the artist! The only constants are Kathleen Ferrier, Elisabeth Schwarzkopf and Nellie Melba. Ah well, one can live in hope . . .

With my very deepest affection and appreciation,

Ever,

BRIGITTE FASSBAENDER

The Wigmore is a unique and magical hall and without doubt, one of the finest chamber music venues in the world.

It has played a huge part in The Nash Ensemble's programming adventures, the Ensemble having first performed in the Hall in 1968, giving many individual concerts and subsequently presenting an annual themed series from 1979. My own personal involvement dates back to the early

fifties, when as a young piano student I had the privilege of playing in this wonderful venue.

What makes it so special is a combination of the joy of music making in an acoustic which is both warm and receptive, for a truly discerning and friendly audience; the awareness of the Hall's famous history, with concerts performed by generations of great soloists and chamber music groups, the knowledge that the Nash is part of this amazing heritage and hopefully its future.

Many thanks too for the extraordinary dedication and vision of its current Director William Lyne and its devoted staff.

Here's to the next hundred years!

AMELIA FREEDMAN, *The Nash Ensemble*

In February 1994 I sang Lieder by Hanns Eisler in a tiny theatre in Brussels. The far from numerous audience included, unbeknown to me, a distinguished, cultured and dedicated man, who afterwards introduced himself as William Lyne and told me how much he had enjoyed the concert and how much the music had impressed him. Only in the course of our brief conversation did it become apparent to me that I was speaking to the Director of the Wigmore Hall. I can say that this was to become one of the most consequential encounters in my artistic life.

A few months later I gave my first song recital at London's Wigmore Hall. The launch of the career as Lieder singer had begun.

I will never forget the first impression of the atmosphere which prevailed during that concert. Up to that moment I had never been faced with such an interested, open-minded, expert and attentive audience. Since then I have been linked through a very intense, pleasant and regular collaboration with Wigmore Hall. All this is no mere accident – it results from years of work due entirely to one Bill Lyne and his team. This work has always been characterised by vision, creativity and adventure. May it ever remain so.

I would like to thank Bill Lyne, Wigmore Hall and their audience,
Your

MATTHIAS GOERNE

It is hard to describe how much the Wigmore Hall means to those who love it. (Arguably) the greatest concert hall in (arguably) the most musically vital city in the world, the beauty of its acoustic is (luckily) beyond argument. It is not only the acoustic, however, that gives the Wigmore its special place in the hearts of those who frequent its concerts (facing either way); still more unique is the atmosphere of the Hall. It is as if the ghosts of great performances, of elated audiences, live on in the Wigmore's unruffled world. Strange that bustling Oxford Street is only a couple of minutes away; the Wigmore inhabits a different era, a different ethos, a different region of the soul.

It is annoying to think that the sun is eating itself up at such a rate that in a few million years its heat will destroy our planet – a thoroughly insensitive way to behave, I must say. We can only hope and trust that the Wigmore Hall will continue to flourish right up to the last. Of course, some might predict that by then man's ingenuity could stretch to creating an exact replica on a distant star; but no – that would be beyond the capabilities of even the most brilliant of genetic engineers. The hall might look the same, even sound the same, but the magic would be missing. So let us content ourselves by making the most of our beloved Wigmore for the next few million years.

Steven Isserlis

Editor's note: It is worth quoting the correspondence I had with Steven Isserlis about his contribution:

'My only query is *eating*? That is definitely what you wrote but do you mean *heating*? The latter would seem more likely to me, though I don't know much about the sun . . .'

'I *do* mean *eating*, not *heating* – as I gather, that's how we survive – the sun eating itself up gives us heat, which gives us life, which gives us the Wigmore!'

Those of us who are fortunate enough to spend our lives playing in concert halls all over the world soon find that all but a handful of locations can swiftly combine into a splendid blur. Life as a travelling musician involves fleeting moments in airports, city centres, hotels (are there stories about those!), artist Green Rooms, concert platforms, restaurants (good and bad) and brief encounters with audiences, that afterwards it's

often difficult to remember clearly too many relevant details. Recently I flew into a major European city which my cellist assured me she had never before visited. Next day we played our concert, but it was only afterwards, when we stopped in a little café, that she remembered that she had played in the same hall just three weeks earlier!

Not so, Wigmore Hall! For there are a few halls which one does not forget. 'The Wigmore', whoever you talk to, performer or audience member, holds a special magic. For those of us on the stage there is a wonderful intimacy with the audience: how 550 people can feel so close is always a delightful mystery to me. The acoustic is a joy: natural, yet enhancing sounds, whether vocal or instrumental, with just the right amount of bloom, but never losing clarity. Backstage it is an extraordinary feeling to be surrounded by mementos of all those great performers: dozens and dozens of photos of the familiar – and occasionally the neglected. I am always drawn towards the portrait of the remarkable French pianist Cécile Chaminade: she was also no mean composer. Tippett's eyes twinkle mischievously as you head out to the stage, whilst Britten keeps a stern, headmasterly eye on those changing and warming up.

I have lost count of how many concerts I have played at Wigmore Hall since I first appeared there seventeen years ago. Certainly it is well over fifty, making it by a long way my most familiar concert haunt anywhere in the world, yet there is still a real magic, a real sense of anticipation, every time I step out onto the stage.

Happy birthday, Wigmore Hall. And may the affection in which you are held, right across the globe, continue through your next hundred years.

ROBERT KING, *The King's Consort*

The Wigmore Hall is the god-mother of music. It looks after and supports the careers of the young up-and-comers and introduces great artists from around the world to London audiences. That audience knows its stuff.

My first visit to the illustrious hall was in the early 60s. A friend of mine had two tickets for a master class being given by the great singer Lotte Lehmann, who I believe was retired from the profession. The class was a revelation. As each singer got up to sing for the diva, she first put them at their ease and then set to work. I swear that at the end of each piece they sang she had, through her sheer knowledge of the work, brought about a small miracle for each one. Every singer left the stage with a big grin while the audience nodded approval. Yet Lotte herself hardly sang a note; she '*talkedsang*'.

Sitting there in awe, it never entered my mind that one day I would be up on that stage being embraced by the beautiful Wigmore godmother.

DAME CLEO LAINE

The name Wigmore Hall was uttered in hallowed tones in our household during my boyhood, and to be asked to help organise a jazz series there was an invitation to shape the musical history of the famous concert venue. My son Alec and I were conscious from the start of the Hall's natural acoustic, and for most of the concerts amplification was conspicuous by its absence, as were drums and heavy percussion instruments. We were proud to give such revered jazz names as Marian McPartland, Billy Taylor, Clark Terry and many others their first opportunity to perform at Wigmore – a setting for intimate jazz that is hard to beat.

JOHN DANKWORTH

Of the many wonderful words the Marschallin sings in *Der Rosenkavalier* the line that upsets me most is not the one about stopping all the clocks, but her puzzlement that she was the young girl, that she will be the old woman, and yet she remains just the same person. I was quite a young woman when I gave my first recital at the Wigmore Hall in 1974. Inside I haven't changed much: I'm still beset by nerves before every concert, but I think the Wigmore Hall has changed quite a lot! The acoustics are as excellent as ever, and cast a golden glow over the sounds produced on the stage, but I remember thinking that the building was rather old, gloomy and dusty and slightly sad. Now thanks to William Lyne's inspired management, it is young, vibrant and lively – and usually packed.

The concerts that stay in my memory as extra-special events are those with Graham Johnson's Songmakers' Almanac, an idea which Bill Lyne encouraged and nurtured. The very first one, devised for Richard Jackson and me, was a catalogue of songs and readings about human vices: laziness, smoking, drinking, etc! It took the audience quite by surprise: it was unusual to be allowed to laugh in the Wigmore Hall!

I always loved singing with Richard, and with Ann Murray and Anthony Rolfe Johnson, the other founder members of the Songmakers' Almanac. We did so many happy concerts together at the Wigmore. As a result of one Ann and I did in 1980, 'If Fiordiligi and Dorabella had been Lieder singers . . .' a duet partnership was born which has taken us all over the world.

One Wigmore concert deeply engraved in my memory was the 'Lieder Capriccio' which Graham devised for me, using the songs of Richard Strauss, and basing the recital on the structure of the opera *Capriccio*. It was quite brilliant, and was scheduled for the 2nd December, 1988. My father died, unexpectedly, in the early hours of December 1st, with my mother and me by his bed. So many of the songs in that programme seemed unbearably apt: *Befreit, Die Nacht*. Certainly it was the hardest concert I have ever done, but I was helped through it by the kindness and understanding of all the marvellous people who work at the Wigmore; it's a great family.

Graham celebrated many of his personal heroes in concerts at the Wigmore Hall: tributes to Peter Pears, Hugues Cuenod, and one I remember vividly was an 80th birthday concert for Gerald Moore. Graham invited the great man on to the stage at the end: he upstaged us all by gesturing to the frieze on the wall behind us and saying, 'It has been some years since I posed for that.'

DAME FELICITY LOTT

After leaving the Royal Academy of Music in 1995, my career seemed to be progressing as fast as one could decently hope for. However, in July two years later, my success in the Cardiff Singer of the World competition accelerated things alarmingly. Then, at the age of 27, riding high on the aftermath of Cardiff, I received a phone call asking whether I would consider stepping in for an indisposed Simon Keenlyside to give a recital in the Wigmore Hall. In my euphoric state at the time I think I almost screamed 'YES!' into the receiver. As to the repertoire, why not *Winterreise*? Malcolm Martineau had persuaded me to learn it earlier that year and, well, it seemed like a good idea at the time.

The next morning reality intruded into Nirvana. That evening I was to sing Schubert's great bottomless masterpiece at barely 24 hours' notice in one of the world's great shrines of recital singing. My only other experience of the Hall at that time was one terrifying audition before what seemed like the assembled crowned heads of musical Europe and an extremely ill-fated foray into the Kathleen Ferrier competition. So, screwing my courage to whatever I could, Malcolm nursed me through the rehearsal. There was then little else to be done.

I remember so vividly walking out onto the stage that evening. The big curved door being held open and walking through onto polished wood. There before me a full hall, it is amazing how close everyone seems, and a tumult of applause. It can only have lasted for twenty or thirty seconds, but to me it was endless. I was so overwhelmed by the welcome I received I was damned if the audience weren't going to have something to applaud at the end. It seemed that many of those there had been watching BBC2 that July, and I was adamant that I should live up to their expectations. During the performance I felt immediately relaxed by both venue and audience. Purely technically the Wigmore is a dream to sing in and with a public so famously knowledgeable and attentive it is as rewarding vocally as it is artistically.

With the benefit of a few years to calm down, I now look back on my impromptu debut with as much delight as I look forward each time to returning. It was a special night for me and will be with me forever.

CHRISTOPHER MALTMAN

Why is the Wigmore Hall the best chamber hall in the world?

Perhaps it is because there are no jagged edges to the people or the environment. Even the oval shape of the stage makes you feel like you're being held in the palm of a very large comforting hand. You walk onto the stage and the platform is high enough so that the audience are not frighteningly close but they are near enough to smile at you and for you to smile back!

You are always aware of all the great performances that have happened in the Hall, but not in an intimidating way. It seems that you are joining the stream that has been flowing so well for so long and that enables you to do your very best. Backstage you are treated with as much respect whether it's your first or fortieth concert.

I love certain quirks in the concert routine; drawing the red curtain behind you just before you walk on, so that the audience gets a more elegant view! William invariably comes back to see you just before the concert begins to offer encouraging noises. You then have to time your walk onto the stage in order that he has time to get back to his seat. He has not lost any speed over the years!

The Wigmore has felt like my artistic home since I started in this mad profession and I'm sure it will progress and still maintain its wonderful traditions in equal proportions for and through the next century.

MALCOLM MARTINEAU

I have been turning up to sing at the Wigmore Hall since I was a student and because you are so wonderful I have never been turned away. I love singing there and feel very much at home.

I have been honoured to be part of the Songmakers' series in this hallowed hall with the painting of Gerald Moore above us, or so he informed us.

Happy, happy celebrations! I hope to be part of your next century.

With love to you all.

ANN MURRAY

There are relative degrees of difficulty. Believe me, I would far prefer to sing this message than write it!

In my long career, the Lied has played a very important part in my work and it all began at the Wigmore Hall. In 1961, I sang *Der Hirt auf dem Felsen* of Franz Schubert. I was 20. In 1971, I made my first ever recording, *Margaret Price at the Wigmore Hall*. Some years later, came what every Lieder singer longs for, a full-length recital at this splendid Hall. Oh the nerves! It began with breakfast, rehearsal at the Hall and the bathroom for the rest of the day! Over all the years this procedure has never changed. Why did the Wigmore Hall have this reaction on my nervous system? No possible reason can be given, since after I had sung the first few notes, all my recitals were the happiest of experiences.

Over the years, William Lyne has developed an audience who know that when they attend a performance at this hall, they are going to have a musical experience on a high level. This stems from his choice of artists and the conditions he and his staff give to the artists. Nowhere in the world in my experience, do you know on arrival that you are going to have peace and quiet for three hours to rehearse, without vacuum cleaners buzzing around and other extraneous noises; where you are met with smiles, friendliness, and a pot of tea and the occasional gin and tonic – after the recital, of course!

My heartfelt good wishes to this unique Wigmore Hall on having provided London with the greatest music making over the last hundred years and many thanks from me personally for having had the privilege of standing on its stage over a period of forty years.

DAME MARGARET PRICE

The warm reception which greeted my first appearance at Wigmore Hall took me by surprise. So much for the reserve of the English audience who have taken me to their hearts! The atmosphere there is like performing for friends. I would like you all to know that the feeling is reciprocated. Many happy returns, Wigmore Hall!

ANDREAS SCHOLL

As the first resident artists appointed by the Wigmore Hall we have always been aware of the great honour given to us and of the responsibility this carries. We are deeply grateful for the invitation to contribute to this book. Our international career took off largely as a result of our residency, and our travels have underlined for us the very great esteem in which the Hall is held around the world, both for the integrity of its planning and the calibre of the artists it engages.

Our regular concerts in this most beautiful hall have always provided a special focus for our work, with audiences that are both highly knowledgeable and supportive. Each appearance is a privilege for us.

Škampa Quartet

When a date at the Wigmore Hall appears in our diary we know it's going to be a special day. Arriving in the morning in this beautiful part of London we can be sure that the cheerful welcome will include freshly brewed coffee, served in lovely china, and a total devotion by everyone at the Hall to making the day as easy as possible for us. After a high energy rehearsal we can go our separate ways, enjoy the local restaurants and then relax in the quiet comfort of the plush backstage rooms.

Pacing around at seven o'clock in the Green Room the level of adrenalin is as high as we ever want it to be as our eyes wander around the amazing gallery of distinguished performers from the past. The world's warmest audience is eagerly, even hungrily, waiting, and we desperately want to do our very best. But the butterflies are overactive and the thought occurs: 'Why do we put ourselves through this?'

And then it's time. With perhaps a well-timed private joke from one of us to relax the tension, the door onto the stage opens, the audience greets us like friends returning from a long journey, we hear the first warm sounds of the music and we know the answer.

You could compare the Wigmore Hall to a very fine old instrument. You feel immediately that it is warm, responsive and generous, offering the potential for the utmost range of colour and dynamics, and then, over a period, you find that there is even more to learn about its character and idiosyncrasies. It would not be an exaggeration to describe the Wigmore Hall as a sort of gold standard to which the other halls we visit can only aspire. It has been marvellous to watch William Lyne nurturing the Hall and its audience so sensitively.

We join many other musicians in being able to say that the Wigmore has played a very significant part in our history, from the invaluable opportunities it gave the quartet at the beginning, to the steadfastness through all that a twenty-five year career can bring.

We congratulate the Wigmore Hall on its first hundred years, and we're grateful for the privilege of playing there so often.

TAKÁCS QUARTET

To put my feelings about Wigmore Hall in simplest terms, I know of no other place like it. The world has other halls with fine acoustics (though they are rare, in my experience). But are the atmosphere and design so perfectly conducive to the intimacy of a song recital?

Or, if they are, do these halls sustain, decade after decade, such high standards with respect to richness of activity and programming?

Or, if they do, do they attract an audience that is as enthusiastic and appreciative – an audience so attentive that you can actually *hear* it listening?

Or, do they have a staff that goes so far, through care and support, toward making a recital seem like something vital, something necessary? This is to say nothing of sheer kindness: on one occasion, I brought my then two-year-old daughter to rehearsal, and the staff presented her with a small, stuffed pig. The pig is still with her, known to this day and with great affection as 'Wigmore'.

I've told the story before that Wigmore was the first of the major international halls to engage me as a recitalist. I remember thinking during the course of that first appearance that a recital career at this level was going to be pure heaven. Of course, it wasn't long before I learned that reality is more complicated. That realisation, however, has only made me treasure Wigmore and my visits there all the more.

In short, there is no place I'd rather go to sing a recital, or to hear one.

DAWN UPSHAW

One of the things I most love about coming back to the Wigmore Hall is being able to renew my acquaintance with the collection of artists' photos that hang backstage, not only in the Green Room, but also in the Gerald Moore Room on the first floor. Here, in the accompanists' inner sanctum our great predecessor presides in private state, flanked by four of his favourite singers: Victoria de los Angeles, Elisabeth Schwarzkopf, Elisabeth Schumann (a delightful portrait from 1926, holding her long-haired Pekinese) and Elena Gerhardt. The last is a signed photo from 1907, aged 24, the young beauty's elegant profile crowned by a stupendous Edwardian hat of rich, dark plumes. On another wall, the already unashamed young accompanist stands hatted and coated on a railway platform with one of his early mentors, the tenor John Coates, 'an aristocrat among singers'. On either side of them, Elena Gerhardt again, still elegant at 60, and Cecil Beaton's radiant Kathleen Ferrier, a photo that captures for ever the lustrous beauty that so perfectly matched her voice and unique personality.

Performing often means spending as much time backstage as on the platform, so it is both inspiring and comforting to have the company of so many blessed spirits during the moments before curtain up. Inevitably I have developed old friends to whom I return, especially in the Green Room. Top of my list is Conchita Supervia, the great Spanish mezzo, who died tragically at the age of 41. Here she appears, eternally vivacious and charming, head thrown back as she laughs into the camera, her shoulders draped in a boa of white ostrich feathers (*see page* 135). For style she knocks all the other, more recent, singers on her wall for six, with the possible exception of Tito Gobbi. He, like Elisabeth Schumann, appears with his dog – a beagle this time – and in a broad-brimmed hat, grinning genially across the room towards the pianists in the opposite corner. Among these it is good to see Geoffrey Parsons sharing the honours with a genial Clifford Curzon, a youthful Arthur Rubinstein, Edwin Fischer beetle-browed and Moiseiwitsch, poetic in floppy collar.

Then there are the violinists: Joachim, bearded and patriarchal (from 1904), Ysaÿe (1918) in fleshy profile with astrakhan collar and long flowing hair, Thibaud (1913) young and brooding, Huberman in virtuoso stance. Not far away another of my favourites, Cécile Chaminade (1905) in lace and puffed sleeves poses dreamily at an upright piano with painted scenery. Here too are Hans Richter and Percy Pitt, looking as though about to retire for a quiet cigar, Carl Dolmetsch and Joseph Saxby brylcreemed and in tails like extras in a Fred Astaire movie. In fact the variety of dress and presentation is impressive, especially compared with today's relatively more relaxed idiom, which may be more audience-friendly, but definitely lacks the class of the stars of old. Take string quartets. The Smetana on the steps of the concert hall in Prague are very jolly with their raincoats and cello cases, but give me any day either of the two pictures of the Léner Quartet; the one a montage of head-and-shoulders portraits on a black background, the other more relaxed but in identical, high-buttoned Al Capone suits.

It has become a private ritual for me to say hello to these and other old friends – Elisabeth Söderström for instance, Michael Tippett, or Benjamin Britten and Peter Pears (in the Red House garden). Or Pears again, captured hauntingly by Malcolm Crowthers after Britten's death, standing at his mantelpiece and gazing rather grimly into the distance past Ben's portrait. But the one photo I never go on stage without acknowledging is the glorious, captivating image of Supervia. I doubt if I am the only one.

ROGER VIGNOLES

The Wigmore Hall has always been a very special place for me. During my time as a student at the Guildhall it was, as a regular member of the audience, where I learned to love recitals and discovered the breadth of wonderful and exciting repertoire. It was also the venue of my own very first recital, and many years on it continues to be a privilege to sing in such a visually and acoustically wonderful venue to such a warm and knowledgeable audience. Happy Centenary!

ANNE SOFIE VON OTTER

'I dreamt I dwelt in marble halls,' says the ballad singer and I have been fortunate, for the Wigmore's magnificent, marbled environs have been my home for nearly half of its century, first as a student in the auditorium and after as one of that privileged group of performers who have been lucky enough to grace its stage.

Memories crowd in: debut recital with Roger, a white chiffon gown dusted with crystals, sparkling in the soft, rose-tinted spotlight, and a garland of encores; countless Songmakers' Almanacs, especially Graham's moving tribute to Peter Pears with the 'tenor man' himself on stage; Christmas Crackers, with the legendary Hugues Cuenod, the Cats' Duet spontaneously becoming a stream of innuendo and invective about our hapless pianist (Roger), and, more recently, coming out after 'I'm dreaming of a white Christmas' to find snow falling in Wigmore Street; a cornucopia of chamber music programmed with consummate skill by Amelia for The Nash Ensemble, Fauré's own haunting arrangement of *La bonne chanson* being my own special favourite; the opening of the refurbished Hall with everyone in the line-up for Vaughan Williams's *Serenade to Music*; Jerome Kern's 'Bill' for William's surprise 30th anniversary evening (*see page* II2); my birthday concert with Graham at the piano for Schubert's *Ständchen* backed by a male voice chorus made up of students, old friends from college days at the RCM, and my husband, all trooping up on-stage from the audience arrayed in lurid bow ties!

The Wigmore is the prince of 'small halls', a veritable jewel with its perfect acoustics, perfect size, and above all, perfect audiences nurtured by years of superlative concert planning, now supremely knowledgeable, generous, eager to be pleased and to be moved, always keeping pace with the performer, so that a mere twinkle in the eye is enough to invite them to join in with soft, melodious tones for a final encore of 'Just a song at twilight' – the stuff of dreams indeed.

SARAH WALKER

Here are the words of 'Bill' as sung on that memorable evening –

OUR BILL (performed by Sarah Walker and Malcolm Martineau)

He's not an Isaacs, a Christie or a Snowman,
Nor yet a showman – no way,
But skilful as Sol Hurok
When bureaucracy's in the way;
His style is a much quieter thing
Than the splash or the dash of a Rudolf Bing,
But if you've need of a man to plan
A harmonic series, he's your man:

He's just our Bill, an Antipodean boy,
But his vision raised the Wigmore from down under;
With Pears and Bream,
And all the cream,
From Lupu to Perahia
From Bär to Holzmair,
So join with me – you surely must agree
That there's a way where you've a Will –
We love him, because he's wonderful,
Because he's just our Bill.

Roger Vignoles

ALAN BLYTH

A Critic at the Wigmore Hall

Picture the Wigmore Hall almost fifty years ago when I first entered its portals. It still had the aura and feeling of its Edwardian past, and many in the usually small audiences seemed redolent of that age or at least of the 1920s and 30s – staid, a bit frumpish, far removed from what we see and hear around us today. Most recitals were given by eager and anxious beginners who had booked the Hall in order to get a notice in *The Times* and/or the *Daily Telegraph*. These sparsely attended occasions, with the likes of Joan Chissell or William Mann of *The Times*, Richard Capell and David Money of the *Telegraph* (often communing with each other in loudish tones on the merits or otherwise of the performer in question) contrasted starkly with the few occasions when a Victoria de los Angeles or Peter Pears was on the platform, and a certain distinction was there for all to hear.

As far as I can recall, in those, for me, far-off, pre-critical days, I usually attended to hear some legendary singer of the pre-war era whom I had known only from the gramophone. I remember the tall, still handsome figure and sensitive art of Keith Falkner, and the grand person and even more rotund voice of his eminent contralto (as mezzos were then called) colleague Muriel Brunskill, a formidable presence, handbag plonked on the piano lid, and all.

When I began attending the Hall regularly in the early sixties,

Bernadette Greevy

things were very much as they had been in the previous decade. As a comparatively youthful critic, I took the cynicism of senior colleagues about debutantes in good part, while ever hoping for some real revelation from a talented newcomer. Such a one I vividly recall was the Irish mezzo Bernadette Greevy (March 1964), who assembled a large audience and was justifiably rewarded with a tremendous reception. Then there were already-established artists such as the late lamented Ilse Wolf to delight with her refined art. The sensitive baritone and Spanish specialist Frederick Fuller appeared with a talented student of his.

WIGMORE HALL

Janet Baker

Gerald Moore

THURSDAY 22nd APRIL 7.30 p.m.

The Kathleen Ferrier Memorial Recital, 1965

An even more distinguished singer, Eleanor Steber, arrived from the USA, by now rather large of girth and a formidable personality (as I discovered one night when she was in the audience) for three exceptionally rewarding recitals. But perhaps most memorable of these long-ago recitals was the first of three given by Cesare Valletti, that most sophisticated and intelligent of Italian tenors, who sang Alessandro Scarlatti, Poulenc, Falla and Pizzetti with distinction and feeling. What a pity he gave up singing all too soon to become a businessman.

Then there was Janet Baker about to reach the zenith of her considerable career. On one memorable occasion in 1965, commemorating Ferrier, she sang Purcell, Mozart (Sesto's 'Parto, parto' – unforgettable in conviction and technical assurance), Schubert and Fauré in her own inimitable way. Later that year there was a Kirckman recital by her of Berlioz

The Kathleen Ferrier Memorial Recital
to commemorate the Tenth Anniversary of the Scholarship Fund

Solitude	PURCELL
Alleluia	
Parto, parto, ma tu ben mio	MOZART
(Clemenza di Tito)	

Heimliches Lieben	SCHUBERT
Abendröthe	
Der Sieg	
Abendstern	
Auflösung	
Gondelfahrer	

INTERVAL

A Northumbrian Sequence	PETER ASTON
(first London Performance)	
Pure I was	
See, the clear sky	
Let in the wind	
Him I praise with my mute mouth of light	

Au pays où se fait la guerre	DUPARC
Soupir	
Après un rêve	FAURE
Rêve d'amour	
Aurore	
Notre amour	

Management : Ibbs & Tillett Ltd.

cover photograph: Douglas Glass.

programme price two shillings

Janet Baker's programme

and Wolf, equally individual, a programme shared with a harpsichordist Virginia Black, of notable promise never quite fulfilled.

And who remembers now that the legendary pianist Martha Argerich made her London debut at the Wigmore in 1965 – Schumann, Chopin and Prokofiev executed with a combination of brilliance and artistry that is natural, cannot be learnt? A pianist of a very different kind, the great accompanist Gerald Moore, ended his distinguished career the following year in *Winterreise* with Derek Hammond-Stroud. Even in those days, period performance wasn't ignored. Frans Brüggen was present in 1966 to play the recorder with distinction.

An even more ground-breaking occasion occurred in July 1966 when John Eliot Gardiner's Monteverdi Choir gave its first London concert. I am glad to say that I was able to recognise their worth in a programme that released the soul of Monteverdi's music and announced Gardiner's skills in persuading choirs to provide an electrifying sound. Sitting, I seem to remember, in the balcony on this occasion, not in the customary critical seats in the stalls, I thought we were part of a prophetic evening where Gardiner was concerned. Since then so many period-instrument groups have appeared in the Hall, among the more recent Florilegium and the Akademie für Alte Musik Berlin.

In my early days at the Hall there was not quite the camaraderie that pertains today in the audience, not that feeling of a shared experience, but even then – indeed I would imagine, since its inception – the Wigmore has been a very special place in which to perform music: its size, its shape, its peculiarly endearing ambience, its cosiness have engendered a feeling of intimate music making among friends that will remain with all the regulars of every generation all their lives.

As the Hall gradually – under William Lyne's dynamic and intelligent direction – began to be the place where so many well-known artists wanted to leave their calling card, there was, inevitably, a small price to pay. With these singers and players occupying so many dates, the debutants have by and large been eased out. That has had the happy consequence that some evenings of excruciating performance, attended by a sparse audience made up almost entirely of friends of the performer and the odd critic, have gone. On the other hand, the chance to greet an unexpected talent of outstanding promise still remains, through the concerts presented in the enterprising Young Masters series.

The 1970s and early 80s saw a heap of both hails and farewells. Among the valedictory events was Pears's memorable recital with Murray Perahia. Since appearing in the Hall to give the legendary première (before even my time!) of Britten's *Michelangelo Sonnets* in 1945, Pears had been a frequent visitor, and always welcome. With Perahia as partner he seemed to take on a new lease of life.

Régine Crespin

Wigmore Hall
Manager: William Lyne
Lessee: The Arts Council of Great Britain

Song Recital Series

Wednesday 17 February 1982 at 7.30pm

Régine Crespin
soprano

Geoffrey Parsons
piano

Arts Council
OF GREAT BRITAIN

Régine Crespin, a legend in herself, gave what were to be her farewell recitals. Nobody could pretend the voice was what it once was, but the interpretations and personality were undiminished, and she left an indelible impression – and had her audience almost in tears. They don't quite make them like that any more.

When Sena Jurinac returned, a voice from the gallery greeted her with a heartwarming 'We've missed you!' and she did not disappoint him or us. Ever chary of recitals – in which she felt naked without a costume – she poured out one last time in London those gloriously rich, enveloping sounds and moved the heart in that eloquent way that made her such a unique artist.

Luigi Alva and Graziella Sciutti, two singers from southern climes who had adorned Glyndebourne for many seasons, returned to acclaim, the charm of their manner and the distinction of their style a pleasure for the connoisseur of refined art. Both were supreme conjurors with the Italian language.

Wigmore Hall
Wigmore Street, W1
Manager: William Lyne

Gerald Moore drawn by Dietrich Fischer-Dieskau

MOORE'S YOUNG ALMANAC

A song biography of Gerald Moore, Patron of the Songmakers' Almanac, in celebration of his 80th birthday.

Felicity Lott soprano
Anthony Rolfe Johnson tenor
Richard Jackson baritone
Graham Johnson piano

Wednesday 1st August 1979 at 7.30pm

Gerald Moore's eightieth birthday programme

Last but very much not least there was Gerald Moore's eightieth birthday programme on a very hot August evening in 1979. The veteran accompanist, long since retired, was delighted by the programme planned by his most congenial successor, Graham Johnson, and made a typically witty speech at the close in which he pretended not to remember Johnson's name by referring to a piece of paper when he spoke it. That endeared him one last time to his many admirers.

Of course, Johnson himself was fast becoming the spirit of song in the Hall. His ground-breaking Songmakers' Almanac soon made the sensible journey from aseptic Purcell Room to user-friendly Wigmore, and delighted the group's huge following with his scrupulously prepared, seemingly inexhaustible programmes. Those, often more than one concert, devoted to a single poet or composer were especially remarkable and of course Felicity Lott, Ann Murray, Anthony Rolfe Johnson and Richard Jackson, the original quartet, supplemented by many other notable singers, gave us as rich, rare and varied a fare of song as has ever been heard in London, or most probably, anywhere. That was a new departure, and one that earned a large and faithful following. Of course, Johnson has also appeared, and continues to do so, with almost every distinguished singer who visits the Hall.

Among faces and voices that soon won the hearts of the public was Brigitte Fassbaender. No longer a young artist when she first appeared, she soon convinced everyone of her very particular and individual powers of execution and communication, and for more than ten years, her recitals were red-letter evenings. Her sudden decision to retire deprived us of a singular and vital talent.

Another new artist with equally arresting attributes was Sergei Leiferkus, whose first recital alerted those present to a talent and intelligence quite out of the ordinary, able, like Fassbaender, to create his own 'theatre' in the context of song. Neither was for the weak of heart: both were (and, in Leiferkus's case are) idiosyncratic and unforgettable.

Another baritone of a different kind who won hearts at his first appearance was the Swedish Håkan Hagegård. A singer of immense charm and with a mellifluous voice to match, he sang Lieder with an irresistible lilt and poise. Just a little later, Olaf Bär first appeared at the Hall having won the Walther Gruner Lieder Competition (now sadly defunct). He immediately established himself as a Lieder interpreter of significance, and his programmes over the following years have always been ones to cherish. Yet a third baritone, Wolfgang Holzmair from Austria, burst upon the scene almost unheralded and at once engrossed his audience with his alternately plangent and dramatic readings. Once joined to Imogen Cooper, that most discerning of pianists, his interpretations grew further in stature, leading to many cherished recordings.

Geoffrey Parsons

Among sopranos Barbara Bonney has stood out for her forthright, un-varnished art. Like so many singers, she owed so much to the late, lamented Geoffrey Parsons, whose tireless work and polished finger-craft were always sympathetic to the style of the artist he was partnering. Roger Vignoles is another in the same class and another who often has helped in devising programmes. One that it would be hard to overlook was called 'The Sea' and, in the company of Thomas Allen and Sarah Walker, two stalwarts of the Hall, evoked the elements with tremendous panache. To the names of Parsons and Vignoles must be added those of Malcolm Martineau and Julius Drake.

So, almost without us quite realising it, the Wigmore had become a place essential to visit for all who wanted to hear the best in singing – and not only singing. Pianists of the calibre of András Schiff and Imogen Cooper made it their preferred venue. Quartets of the status of the Lindsay and Takács have made the Hall their London home.

Soon yet another generation of singers was upon us. Ian Bostridge electrified audiences with his here-and-now interpretations in which he becomes the protagonist in the songs of Schubert, Schumann and Britten. Much the same should be said of the baritone Matthias Goerne.

Leif Ove Andsnes   *Dmitry Hvorostovsky*

Then Christine Schäfer has won plaudits for her fastidious art, the very epitome of *Innigkeit*. And the Russians send us more and more exciting artists – Hvorostovsky, Borodina and now the astonishing Larissa Diadkova, while, in the pianist's field, the Norwegian Leif Ove Andsnes demands attention at his every appearance.

The Wigmore, which in my earliest days, was mostly peopled by a, to put it politely, mature audience is now a venue where music lovers of all ages congregate. The only thing most of its members have in common is a true love of the art of music and its executants. Discussion of the differing merits of respective singers or instrumentalists is always lively, often disputatious. And loyalty to the Wigmore and all it represents surely will have some readers take me to task for missing this or that outstanding event so I apologise in advance, for any and every omission.

I shall end with another and important aspect of the Hall's activities and that is the competitions held there. It has been home to the Kathleen Ferrier Memorial Prize since its inception in the 1950s, to the Richard Tauber Prize for some 25 years and recently to the Wigmore Hall International Song Competition. These events often disclose talents for the future – though perhaps it is worth remarking that neither Janet Baker nor Ian Bostridge won first prize in the Ferrier in the years they competed! – but that they did compete and got a feeling for singing at the beloved Wigmore is surely a justification in itself for that and the other events.

So happy centenary, old friend. May the second 100 years be as fruitful and memorable as have been the first.

A

B

C

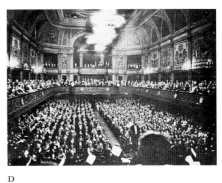

D

E

F

G

A *Vienna, Grosser Musikvereinsaal* 1870
B *Basle, Stadt Casino* 1876
C *Glasgow, St Andrew's Hall* 1877
D *Leipzig, Neues Gewandhaus* 1886
E *Amsterdam, Concertgebouw* 1888
F *Zurich, Grosser Tonhallesaal* 1895
G *Boston, Symphony Hall* 1900

DEREK SUGDEN

The Wigmore Hall and its Acoustic

The years from 1870-1900 were the 'golden age' for the European concert hall. Vienna, Grosser Musikvereinsaal 1870; Basle, Stadt Casino 1876; Glasgow, St Andrew's Hall 1877; Leipzig, Neues Gewandhaus 1886; Amsterdam, Concertgebouw 1888; Zurich, Grosser Tonhallesaal 1895; and then across the Atlantic to Boston, Symphony Hall 1900. Although the New World's first 'genuine concert hall', it followed strictly the precepts of the European concert hall, with its rectangular plan, side and end balconies and a flat ceiling.

Those seven great halls are invariably described as 'shoe-box' halls. In addition to their rectangular geometry, they were heavily moulded and highly decorated, which provided high levels of diffusion of the sound. In addition to the side balconies, there was invariably choir seating behind the orchestral platform, which was occupied by the audience when no choir was present. The one exception amongst these seven great halls is Boston which encloses the orchestra within a proscenium arch, an Italian opera house influence, which is seen in many American halls.[1]

The Wigmore Hall, opened in 1901, followed this European tradition of the 'shoe-box' with its rectangular geometry, though appreciably smaller than these great halls. Apart from being on a smaller scale, it has two significant differences. The surfaces of the Wigmore Hall are plain with a minimum of diffusing elements and the ceiling is a barrel vault. The interior is quite severe, but includes a frieze of red Verona marble around the entire room with a dado of Caribbean mahogany panelling. The platform is enclosed by an alcove with circular geometry surmounted by a cupola with a coloured bas-relief which is the most striking part of the auditorium.[2] This platform geometry with its radius centre, just

1. There is also a suggestion of proscenium separation in St Andrew's Hall, Glasgow, where the cornice was returned across the hall and supported by 2 classical columns.
2. The artist for the bas-relief was Gerald Moira who worked with Collcutt and who,

within the main Hall and approximately coinciding with the centre of the platform, will give a certain degree of focussing to the front side seats and excellent conditions for chamber groups to hear each other and encourage ensemble playing. Otherwise the architecture is quite restrained. The plain plastered walls are broken only by shallow pilasters and the plastered ceiling is broken by a small definition of the ribs of the roof structure and a simple laylight.

There are certain precedents for smaller 'shoe-box' halls with similar plain surfaces which lack diffusion combined with ceilings of curved geometry. The most famous being the concert room in Eisenstadt, often referred to as the Haydn-Saal, although it was built in 1700 some 32 years before Haydn's birth.

The Eisenstadt room is 38m x 14.7m x 12.4m high. Wigmore Hall is 23m x 12.5m x 10m (average height). There is no fixed seating in the Eisenstadt room, but Professor Jürgen Meyer who has measured and calculated many of the halls associated with Haydn has measured the room with 300 chairs and from these measurements has calculated a reverberation time when occupied of 1.7 seconds.[3]

The Wigmore Hall has 548 seats when measured from the architect's drawing, 466 on the main floor, with 78 in the balcony. With spaces for the disabled the box office give the figures as 463 and 76, together with a few standing places.

Like Eisenstadt, the volume of air per seat is ideal for creating a great chamber hall acoustic. Apart from the audience who virtually cover the carpet and seats, there are no absorbing surfaces in the Hall. The acoustic accommodates chamber groups with ease and elegance, it is both loud and clear and achieves that elusive balance between clarity and reverberance which is lacking in so many halls. Measurements taken before and after the renovation and refurbishment of 1991 to 1992, including the stage and piano lift and without an audience, show a mid-frequency reverberation time of 1.75 seconds when empty [*Fig* 1]. Allowing for the

from 1890, was Professor of Art at the Royal College of Art. The relief represents 'The Genius of Harmony' with 'The Soul of Music' radiating down to earth but is separated from the four earthly figures by a barrier of thorns.

3. Professor Jürgen Meyer: *Joseph Haydn: His Concert Halls – His Orchestra – His Symphonies*. Lecture held at the ESTA Meeting at Eisenstadt, Austria in 1982.

Eisenstadt, Haydn-Saal 1700

Wigmore Hall 1901 looking towards stage   *Wigmore Hall looking towards balcony*

absorption of an audience on upholstered seats and carpet, this indicates an occupied reverberation time of 1.6 seconds which is ideal for chamber music in a hall of this size.

A quiet background is essential to achieve a great acoustic. Acousticians now pay great attention to the design of mechanical services and to the design and construction of the fabric of the building to achieve these

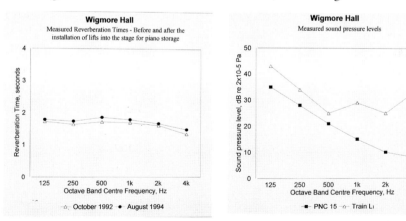

Fig 1. Reverberation time measurement before and after the renovation work of 1991-2, including the stage and piano lift. Hall unchanged and unoccupied.

Fig 2. Curve showing noise levels of underground train plotted against PNC15 curve.

very low ambient noise levels, so important in enabling musicians to achieve a real *ppp* and so improve the dynamic range and impact of the music. This has been achieved in modern auditoria, and particularly, in Birmingham Symphony Hall, Glyndebourne Opera House and Bridge-water Hall.

The acoustics of many old halls suffer from poor sound insulation and noisy mechanical ventilation and air conditioning. The Wigmore Hall has a generally quiet background with good protection from street noise. There is some noise penetration through the roof and opening laylight. The underground trains are occasionally audible in quiet passages [*Fig 2*]. These occasional intrusive noises above the generally quiet background do not appear to detract too seriously from the fine acoustic of the Wigmore Hall, apart from its use as a professional recording studio. During the extensions and alterations in 1991-2, an appreciable amount of work was done to the mechanical services below the ground floor. Great care was taken in the design and construction of these services and of the building fabric, to ensure that there were no intrusive noises within the Hall. Measurements showed this to be very successful and there was even a slight decrease in the background noise level [*Fig 3*].

No work was carried out in the main hall during this contract, apart from cleaning and painting. As expected this raised the reverberation time above 500 Hz by a fraction. The measurements showed an average

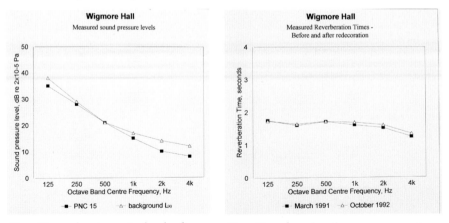

Fig 3. Curve showing noise levels after completion of renovation work in 1991-2 plotted against PNC15 curve.

Fig 4. Reverberation time measurement taken before and after decoration of the main hall. Hall unoccupied.

increase of 0.1 seconds between 500 and 4000 Hz. [*Fig 4*]. It is just possible that young performers and young members of the audience may have noticed a slightly brighter sound!

The absorption of an audience is by far the biggest factor in the measurement of the reverberation time of an enclosed space. The larger the audience the lower the reverberation time, although the absorption of an audience is proportional to its superficial area, rather than to the number seated. The Hanover Square Rooms, famous for the first performance of Haydn's London Symphonies and in use from 1775 to 1874, was recorded as seating between 800 and 900. It had dimensions very similar to the Wigmore Hall. Different authorities give its length between 90 and 79 ft (27m and 24m) and its width between 32 and 30 ft (9.8m and 9m). Prof. Jürgen Meyer calculates a reverberation time with an audience of 800 as being less than 1 second. Whatever the audience numbers, seated or standing, the two rooms are very similar, although Wigmore Hall approaches the double cube, whereas Hanover Square approaches the triple cube. They both had curved ceilings and were very plain and, therefore, lacking in diffusion.

These properties certainly give the Wigmore's acoustic a great distinction. Its curved roof is of elliptical geometry with two foci, well above the audience on the main floor. Those who choose the side seats in the balcony will experience this focus, which gives the music great presence, one of my favourite spots in addition to the side seats towards the front already referred to. One can sit anywhere, however, to experience, for me, the best chamber music acoustic anywhere in the world.

BECHSTEIN HALL.

A..

Grand Concert

UNDER THE PATRONAGE OF

THE ITALIAN EMBASSY,

THE ITALIAN CONSULATE,

THE ITALIAN CHAMBER OF COMMERCE,

IN AID OF THE ITALIAN HOSPITAL

And other Italian Charitable Institutions in London,

WILL TAKE PLACE ON

FRIDAY, 13th JULY, 1906, at 3 o'clock.

Under the direction of
SIGNOR F. PAOLO TOSTI and SIGNOR C. CAMPANINI.

The following Artists have kindly consented to appear :—

* Signora GIACHETTI, * Mlle. DONALDA, and * Mlle. DESTINN
* Mme. KIRKBY LUNN and Signora DENZA
* Signor CARUSO
* Signor SCOTTI, * Signor SAMMARCO, and * Signor BATTISTINI
MISCHA ELMAN
Signor TITO MATTEI and Signor SIMONETTI
Monsieur COQUELIN
Signor DENZA, Signor BARALDI, and Signor BARTHÉLEMY

* By kind permission of the Grand Opera Syndicate.

Prices: Sofa Stalls £1 1s.; Balcony Stalls, 10/6.

COMMITTEE.

CONTESSA DE BOSDARI, 20 Grosvenor Square, W.
CONTESSA CORINALDI, 20 Grosvenor Square, W.
CONTESSA DE VILLAREY, 20 Grosvenor Square, W.
SIGNORA ALBANESI, 3 Gloucester Terrace, Hyde Park, W.
SIGNORA L. ALLATINI, 53 Holland Park, W.
SIGNORA R. ALLATINI, 18 Holland Park, W.
SIGNORA ANGELI, 171 Queen's Gate, S.W.
SIGNORA I. DE MARTINO, 2 College Terrace, Belsize Park, N.W.
SIGNORA DE RIN, 10 Highbury Crescent, N.
SIGNORA GRANCINI, 28 Belsize Square, Hampstead, N.W.
SIGNORA NAUMANN, 12 Bedford Square, W.C.

SIGNORA ORTELLI, 22 Russell Square, W.C.
SIGNORA PEIRANO, 41 Gloucester Gardens, Bishop's Road, W.
SIGNORA PILGRIM, "Carlsbrook," Rosendale Road, Herne Hill, S.W.
SIGNORA POLENGHI, Horley, Surrey.
SIGNORA REITMEYER, "Venezia," Shortlands Grove, Shortlands, Kent.
LADY SAMUELSON, 56 Prince's Gate, S.W.
SIGNORINE MARIA and OLGA SERENA, 36 York Terrace, Regent's Park, N.W.
SIGNORINA SPERATI, "Rosa Alba," Highbury Park, N.
SIGNORA TOSTI, 12 Mandeville Place, W.

Tickets may be had of any of the Members of the Committee and of the following : THE ITALIAN CONSULATE, 44 Finsbury Square, E.C.; THE ITALIAN CHAMBER OF COMMERCE, 4 St. Mary Axe, E.C.; Chappell & Co., 50 New Bond Street; Ashton, 38 Old Bond Street; Keith, Prowse, Cheapside and branches; Cecil Roy, Sussex Place and Branches; Hays, 4 Royal Exchange Buildings, E.C.; and

G. RICORDI & Co., 265 Regent Street;
The BOX OFFICE, Bechstein Hall.

Grand Concert in Aid of the Italian Hospital, 13 July 1906

JOHN STEANE

Singers at the Wigmore Hall

Singers had clearly been in the designer's mind. Both *Musical Times* and *Musical Opinion* made a point of it: the artists' rooms, they noted, were 'on a level with and immediately adjacent to the platform', by which happy arrangement 'singers will not have to arrive breathless on the platform after climbing a flight of stairs'. The inaugural concerts are mentioned but not reviewed by these two leading musical monthlies which give the events a warm welcome but not much space. The great virtuosi, Ysaÿe, Busoni and Pachmann are mentioned as having played; and then it would seem that the first singers to come adjacently forth, their store of the vital element suffering no undue depletion on the way, were Mr Ben Davies and Mr Plunket Greene. In fact the first solo singer (who thus deserves a place in the story even though nothing much more of her seems to be known) was Mme. Helen Trust, who sang *God Save the King*. The other singer at the opening concert on 31 May 1901, was the baritone Raymund von Zur-Mühlen, reputedly among the first singers to have devoted a whole evening's programme to Lieder. On this occasion he sang three songs by Schubert: *Nacht und Träume*, *Der Jüngling an der Quelle* and *Erl-könig*. The English singers appeared at the second concert and were to be back.

Despite the celebrity-laden inaugurals and the adjacent artists' rooms, the new hall did not immediately attract well-known singers, not even the British. Nor were the programmes always such as one associates with the Wigmore today. On 17 June, for instance, Miss Teresa del Riego, composer of the well-known song 'Homing', conducted a concert 'with whistling solos by Mr J. del Riego'. Still, the first season brought (separately) concerts by three celebrated Susans: Susan Metcalfe (later to become Metcalfe-Casals, giving a Wigmore concert under that name in 1922 accompanied by her husband), Susan Adams and Susan Strong, the last two taking time off from the doubtless very high-class laundries which they ran, also separately. Strong, who had been briefly a noted principal soprano at Covent Garden, the Metropolitan and Bayreuth, became a regular visitor, her admirably chosen programmes printed on what looked like a rather elegant visiting-card and notifying the public of her private address at Regent's Park. Her accompanist until his death in 1913 was Francis Korbay, the composer and godson of Liszt. Other accompanists in these early years were Percy Grainger, Hamilton Harty, Landon Ronald and a certain Herr Basche.

Elena Gerhardt

The first real *coup* for the Hall as far as singers were concerned came in the form of an almost legendary baritone who was then resident in London. Victor Maurel, 'creator' of Verdi's Iago and Falstaff, may have even then seemed to belong to another age but in fact did not reach 60 until 1908. He made his Wigmore (or Bechstein) debut in 1905 and returned more than once both that year and the next. Several items, including Iago's 'Creed' and Falstaff's 'Quand' ero paggio', were listed as 'by desire', and in the fourth concert he was 'assisted by his pupil Mrs Robert Menzies'. Other souvenirs of the previous century arrived following this, principally Ernest van Dyck (the original Parsifal and Werther), and the bass Edouard de Reszke.

Perhaps these veterans spread news of the Hall to Covent Garden itself, for on 13 July 1906, celebrities rained upon it like Jove in a shower of gold. A 'Grand Concert in Aid of the Italian Hospital' was planned under the direction of Paolo Tosti and the conductor Cleofonte

Arthur Nikisch

Campanini. Did they all arrive together, one wonders, in a fleet of taxis? Or did they saunter down in voluble groups after luncheon at their favourite restaurant, Pagani's in Great Portland Street? Anyway, there came Caruso, Battistini, Destinn, Kirkby Lunn, Scotti, Sammarco, Donalda, Giacchetti, with the violin prodigy Mischa Elman and the great French actor Coquelin. The programme was a rich casserole of bits-and-pieces and ended with the Quartet from *Rigoletto* sung by Donalda, Lunn, Caruso and Scotti. The *Musical Opinion* article about the Hall at the time of its opening had reckoned that the number of seats (400 downstairs, 100 in the gallery) 'will easily accommodate the largest number of the paying public likely to be attracted'. It would be interesting to know if there were spare seats going that afternoon.

Another team from Covent Garden, but this one a rather Second-Eleven type, followed in November, destined for 'Sig. Denza's morning concert (at 3 pm)', and headed by the tenor Giovanni Zenatello. It was in this year too that Nellie Melba came to the Wigmore, but obviously the Hall's future did not lie in this kind of thing. More significant was the return a few months later of the young mezzo-soprano from Leipzig and her renowned accompanist. Elena Gerhardt and Arthur Nikisch, their programme adorned with quotations from the foreign press, had given their first recital on 13 June 1906. In the next two years and again in 1910 they reappeared for a series which was considered to be among the great occasions in the musical life of London at the time. After the outbreak of war came a long absence and when Gerhardt returned in 1929 (Nikisch had died seven years earlier) it was with the reputation of being the greatest of Lieder singers. She would now give programmes devoted to a single composer, including Wolf just about the time when the famous Society recordings were made. One memorable occasion must have been a Schubert and Brahms recital in 1944 when she shared the platform with Myra Hess as she had so often done at the National Gallery for the lunch-hour concerts in the darkest days of wartime in London. Another took place on 7 November 1943, when Gerhardt celebrated the 40th anniversary of her first Liederabend, given in Leipzig on her twentieth birthday. The programme reproduced two photographs of the singer, one taken in the year of the concert, the other in 1903. Gerhardt's records are no longer fashionable, but it is worth remembering the words of Gerald Moore in his book *Am I Too Loud?*: 'When in these present times a programme of German Lieder fills the large halls of London and New York we should remember Elena Gerhardt and be thankful, for it was her missionary work that did so much to convert the English-speaking world into worshippers of Schubert and his royal succession.'

Another mezzo-soprano who contributed to this end in the early years was Julia Culp, who sang first at the Hall in 1910. The inter-war period brought Elisabeth Schumann (1926-28), Emmi Leisner (1931), Ria Ginster (1933-34) and Gerhard Hüsch (1935-36), who also gave an entire programme, accompanied by Moore, to songs by Yryö Kilpinen. Others gave recitals in which songs were mixed with, and sometimes overwhelmed by, operatic arias. The Heldentenor Leo Slezak arrived in 1927, startling the echoes with Max's solo from *Der Freischütz* for an opening number and putting them to unaccustomed frenzy at the end with his aria from *La Juive*; in between came some Lieder in which the *mezza voce* seemed to belong to a different voice. A soprano who sang her Desdemona to his Otello, Frances Alda, on a rare visit to London in 1907 included arias from *Alceste*, *La traviata* and Catalani's *Loreley*. The previous year Franz Naval, a stylish lyric tenor, followed enterprising choices of Lieder with arias from *Manon* and *La Bohème*. Sydney Raynor (1933) included arias from *Lohengrin* and Mascagni's *Iris*, and Gwen Catley concluded her debut recital in 1939 with the Mad Scene from *Lucia di Lammermoor*. Many gave song recitals with mixed programmes, often German and French as when the delightful Lotte Schöne sang in 1936 and 37, or (a collector's piece, this one) Gabrielle Ritter-Ciampi in 1933. There were visitors from America, among them Dan Beddoe (1911), Richard Crooks (1925), Marian Anderson (1928), Rose Bampton (1936) and, most frequently, Roland Hayes (1919-37), all giving relatively eclectic programmes. In 1921 the great, but then virtually unknown, Lauritz Melchior joined forces with the bass Holgar Hansen: again a mixed programme, with Danish songs, the duet from *Les Pêcheurs de perles*, and an item which must have tested the audience's sense of humour rather severely, a cantata of student life called *Gluntarne* ('very successful' according to the programme). Maria Ivogün ended her 1933 concert with *The Blue Danube*. Czech songs were featured in a programme by Jarmila Novotná

Marian Anderson, 15 June 1928   *Teyte and Cortot, 6 November 1937*

WIGMORE HALL
WIGMORE STREET, W.1

MARIAN
ANDERSON
(CONTRALTO)

Song
Recital

**FRIDAY,
JUNE 15th
at 3.15**

At the Piano:
JOAN SINGLETON

BÖSENDORFER GRAND PIANOFORTE

TICKETS (including Tax): Reserved, 8/6 and 5/9.   Admission, 3/-
May be obtained from the Box Office, Wigmore Hall; the usual Ticket Offices; and of
elephone: Mayfair 4201-2-3
elegrams: " Organol, Wesdo, London."   IBBS & TILLETT, 124, Wigmore Street, W.1.

For Programme, P.T.O.

WIGMORE HALL

MAGGIE TEYTE
AND
CORTOT

DEBUSSY
RECITAL

NOVEMBER 6TH, 1937

STEINWAY PIANOFORTE

PROGRAMME
ONE SHILLING

IBBS & TILLETT
124 Wigmore Street, W.1

(1928), Russian in one by Nina Koshetz, accompanied in 1925 by the composer Grechaninov, and by the great bass Alexander Kipnis in 1937.

French song had its specialists though they were not much in evidence during the inter-war years as might have been expected. Even when Maggie Teyte sang first (1912) there was no Debussy, Fauré or Duparc, only what were then known as 'ballads', with titles such as 'Ashes of Roses' and 'At Parting'. Eventually (1937) she was to give her famous Debussy recital with Alfred Cortot, but meanwhile more in the French repertoire came from Claire Croiza (a frequent visitor), Ninon Vallin (1928), Eidé Norena (1935), Jane Bathori (who introduced the *Bilitis* songs in 1908) and Charles Panzèra (two concerts in 1929).

And then there was Supervia. The adorable Conchita was often to be seen in Wigmore Street where her husband owned a florist's shop only a few steps away from the Hall, in which, in 1933, she gave what may well have been its first all-Spanish song recital, appearing in various national costumes. Another, with Falla's 7 *Popular Songs*, followed in 1934, and all too soon after that came the news of her lamentable death in childbirth.

And what, in all this time, of the British singers for whose use the Hall was no doubt specially intended, and who contributed to its programmes week-in, week-out? The sad truth is that of most of them it is hard to say. Following Mr Ben Davies and Mr Plunket Greene, whose names at least are still almost familiar, innumerable singers trod the boards, many of them once only, the great majority of them unremembered even by those of us who make it our business to care for such things. Some would surely have made a name and had something to show for it on records nowadays. The soprano Dorothy Silk, contralto Anne Thursfield, tenor Steuart Wilson, baritone Mark Raphael (at least three of whom made records) might have constituted a 'Songmakers' Almanac' had there been anyone clever enough to have invented it in the thirties. Several of them were more enterprising in their musical interests than the time encouraged them to be; and of course the Wigmore was just the place where, then as now, an enlightened public could give its support. Among the leading British singers of the century in its early years, John Coates was one of the Hall's 'regulars'. The famous opera singer, Louise Kirkby Lunn, was another who returned, always with well thought-out programmes. Yet among the inter-war singers, or what we might think of as the *Serenade*

Conchita Supervia

to Music generation, many of the obvious names – Isobel Baillie, Elsie Suddaby, Heddle Nash, Norman Allin for instance – rarely if ever turned up on the Wigmore lists. Astra Desmond was one who did, even devoting a whole programme to Grieg. Of the Australians, Peter Dawson came in the twenties with a perhaps surprisingly varied collection of Lieder (his debut dated back to 1910 when he had sung 'Kangaroo and Dingo' in an anti-vivisection concert). Florence Austral gave a nice-looking programme in 1937, ending with 'Pace, pace, mio Dio' from *La forza del destino*; and that I would like to have heard.

But how many Wigmore recitals fall into that category! Even in the period I like to think of as 'mine', so many were missed. That hardly extends back to the war years of the 1940s, but how marvellous, for instance, to have been at the first performance of Britten's *Serenade for Tenor, Horn and Strings*, with Peter Pears and Dennis Brain, Walter Goehr conducting, in 1943. And the following year brought what was announced as the first performance (though I believe there had been an earlier one) by Robert Irwin of Finzi's *Let us Garlands Bring*, surely the best of all Shakespeare cycles. Those were the times too when our Russian allies were popular heroes and the colourful Oda Slobodskaya devoted a concert ('speakers Lady Strabolgi and Barnett Janner') to 'the heroic Russian Army'.

In the post-war years a debut not to be missed was that of Victoria de los Angeles in 1950. The critic Alec Robertson used to tell stories about this – how he had to walk round the block before he could think of going home and then greeting everyone in the bus queue still in the glow of revelation. She soon became a filler of the Festival Hall, but in later years returned to the Wigmore, the voice reduced (like the luxuriance of her thick black hair) but even at the last, when she was almost 70, there would be moments in some of the Spanish songs or perhaps in Carmen's *Seguédille*, daringly sung as a final encore, when the voice of Robertson's delight would reappear.

She, Elisabeth Schwarzkopf and Dietrich Fischer-Dieskau, the singers at Gerald Moore's Farewell Concert in the Festival Hall, were generally thought of as the big fish hardly to be enticed into the Wigmore pool. Fischer-Dieskau indeed never sang there, though in April 2000 he appeared before us to be interviewed by Sir John Tooley in celebration of

Elisabeth Schwarzkopf rehearsing with Gerald Moore

his 75th birthday. Schwarzkopf appeared at the Wigmore first in 1951 and became a regular visitor in the later years of her career. Her return was part of the *mensis mirabilis* in the Hall's own 75th birthday year, when Rubinstein also returned and Pears and Murray Perahia gave their memorable *Dichterliebe*. This was the time when the Hall polished up its image and reasserted itself as a place where the monthly fare might be not merely worthy but also exciting. Of the Schwarzkopf concert, Edward Greenfield's review in the *Guardian* related its success directly to the place and its rightness for such occasions: 'If ever the Wigmore Hall and its acoustic needed a testimonial in sound, this recital from the newly honoured Dr Schwarzkopf was just that. I have long counted Schwarzkopf's rich and varied recitals at the Festival Hall as unique occasions in the concert-going year . . . But listening to her in Wigmore Hall . . . presented a totally different experience . . . Here was Schwarzkopf using every register and every nuance of expression with the daring of a singer half her age.' It was, he said, 'a recital to underline her superior quality in Lieder of making the rare seem familiar and vivid and the familiar seem new and unexpected'. Geoffrey Parsons, 'inspired by the electricity of the occasion', was the excellent accompanist.

After her retirement Schwarzkopf gave a series of master classes, following in the line of some eminent predecessors such as Lotte Lehmann and Hans Hotter. Tito Gobbi and Gérard Souzay were others who were to appear in this role, and more recently Brigitte Fassbaender and Elly Ameling. Favourite singers have also returned as judges on the panels of competitions: Janet Baker, for instance, presented the prizes at the Kathleen Ferrier Awards of 1993. Auditions for the Richard Tauber Award have also been held here, and 1997 saw the inauguration, specially associated with the Hall, of the International Song Competition of which Fischer-Dieskau is patron.

And of course 'singing at the Wigmore' has not invariably meant recitals by a singer and pianist. In the early days the 'Beecham Orchestral Concerts' would sometimes cram an orchestra onto the platform and the singers would contend with that. Or an instrumental ensemble might be involved as in 1922 when the 22-year-old Joan Cross, in what must have been one of her first public appearances, sang Chausson's *Chanson perpétuelle* with the Mandeville String Quartet. In the 1930s the New English Singers (young Peter Pears their second tenor, Eric Greene their first) sang madrigals. Recent times have brought expert groups such as the Tallis Scholars and Gothic Voices. Concerts of mediaeval and renaissance music have involved a team of singers; and in this notable extension of public musical interest the Hall has again taken a full part.

No fuller part in the entire history of music making at the Wigmore has been played by any individual or group than by Graham Johnson's Songmakers' Almanac. Formed in 1976, it consisted originally of four singers – Felicity Lott, Ann Murray, Anthony Rolfe Johnson and Richard Jackson, with Johnson as pianist, organiser and prime source of inspiration. They gave their first concert at the Purcell Room, and came to the Wigmore in 1978. After an 80th birthday concert in honour of Gerald Moore, their patron, and a series of 'Summer Song Cycles' in 1980 the Hall became their artistic home. Other singers have joined over the years, and over the years the programmes have brought surprise-and-delight not as single elements but as a condition of existence. Their 20th anniversary concert, *A Lieder Capriccio*, was subtitled 'Songs by Richard Strauss in a Liederspiel-Quodlibet inspired by his last opera'. Try working on that as a theme! When the Hall had its own anniversary – 90 in 1991 – the Songmakers were ready with a *Nachhall und Widerhall*, being 'Echoes and Reminiscences of the First Season'. The singers on this occasion were Patricia Rozario, Sarah Walker, John Mark Ainsley and (representing the original quartet) Richard Jackson. Of Liza Lehmann's cycle *The Daisy Chain* Graham Johnson remarked that 'the texts show their age rather more than does the Hall.'

This was a reference to the Wigmore's imminent closure for refurbishment – and how we missed it! Since then (eight years at the time of writing) the Hall has resumed business and the singers have been in plentiful supply. These have included the newcomers who are so vividly in the mind's eye at the present, Ian Bostridge and Matthias Goerne perhaps most notably of all. The Russians and Americans have appeared in happy succession (Gorchakova, Borodina, Larin, Hvorostovsky and Leiferkus prominent among the Russians, Fleming, Bonney, Upshaw, Graham and Hampson among the Americans). Most who come once and make a success of it will return, but there have been a few 'one-off' recitals that have proved memorable if controversial: the soprano Alessandra Marc, for instance, deployed her full voice in some operatic arias wherein I rejoiced but others were observed putting cotton-wool in their ears.

Everyone has a store of special memories. Some are of occasions in which the deepest places of a great work have been discovered – I think, for instance, of a *Winterreise* by Peter Schreier and András Schiff in 1995. At the end there was some little doubt in the applause: would it look as though we were asking for an encore? Unthinkable, it seemed. And yet an encore was given, the *Wandrers Nachtlied*, 'Über allen Gipfeln ist Ruh', which seemed the only possible one, absolutely right and a precious experience in itself. There have also been those times when, knowingly or not, we have said goodbye to a great singer who has miraculously sung in a way that perfectly encapsulated the greatness: Christa Ludwig singing Mahler's *Ich bin der Welt abhanden gekommen*, Margaret Price with feeling warm as her magnificent voice in *Der Jüngling und der Tod*, or Nicolai Gedda magical in Tchaikowsky's *At the Ball*. Often encore-time is best of all, not least when something conventionally written-off as worthless proves worthy, as when Felicity Lott chose *Roses of Picardy*. On the whole our audiences do not like too ready an assumption of informality or experimental programming. Yet there have been times too when a formal concert has almost resolved into a family party: Bryn Terfel, after singing Finzi's *Let us Garlands Bring* with a touch of genius, coaxed the audience into supplying a chorus (albeit a decorously murmurous one) to the Flanders and Swann 'Hippopotamus' song.

Sometimes – and I found this at the very last concert I heard before writing this chapter – the presence of a loved singer itself generates the warmth into which the element of magic may find its mysterious way. Thomas Allen, with Roger Vignoles in excellent form, gave a programme of British song with Britten's Hardy settings, *Winter Words*, at the centre. We must have welcomed Sir Thomas (as he now is) time without number, and just as innumerable have been the times when we have left the Hall feeling the better for it. In this concert his voice seemed utterly unchanged, the production was a model for all young singers, and we heard every word. More: he sang to the heart, and Wigmore audiences, experienced and critical as they are, have no objection to that.

*W*IGMORE
HALL

SONG RECITAL SERIES

Tuesday 18 April 2000 at 7.30 pm

SIR THOMAS ALLEN
baritone

ROGER VIGNOLES
piano

PROGRAMME
Would patrons please stifle coughing as much as possible
and ensure that watch alarms, mobile phones and any other
electrical devices which can become audible are switched off

JOHN IRELAND (1879-1962)	If there were dreams to sell
HENRY PURCELL (1659-1695)	Music for a While
REAL. BENJAMIN BRITTEN	Let the dreadful Engines
BENJAMIN BRITTEN (1913-1976)	Winter Words Op 52
	INTERVAL
GUSTAV HOLST (1874-1934)	Three Vedic Hymns Op 24
MICHAEL HEAD (1900-1976)	The Estuary
REBECCA CLARKE (1886-1979)	The Seal Man • Eight O'Clock
CECIL ARMSTRONG GIBBS (1889-1960)	Silver
	English Songs to be announced from the stage

90-93 FM **B B C** RADIO 3
This evening's concert is being recorded for BBC Radio 3
and will be broadcast on 24 April at 7.30 pm

Wigmore Hall Director: William Lyne MBE, Hon. FTCL, Hon. GSM, Hon. RAM, Hon. RCM
Lessees: City of Westminster
The Wigmore Hall Trust • Registered Charity No.1024838
Cover design by Peter Williamson

PROGRAMME: £2.00

Thomas Allen and Roger Vignoles, 18 April 2000

Graham Johnson and the original Songmakers' Almanac: Richard Jackson, Ann Murray, Anthony Rolfe Johnson, Felicity Lott

GRAHAM JOHNSON

Not so much a Programme, more a Way of Life

The opening of every new Wigmore Hall brochure is a delicious experience for recital addicts. As if by magic, promises of feasts-to-come grace every page. Inspired by William Lyne's broader programme suggestions, performers of every kind have slaved away to fill in the details – sequences of alluring menus designed to appeal to those with an appetite for music, London's sonic foodies. To partake of the feast there is no need to buy kitchen implements from Divertimento on the opposite side of the road, and where else can one devour so many courses at a fixed price? Perhaps the food critic of the *Evening Standard* ought to review a Wigmore recital (offending artists pelted, or perhaps drizzled, with rotten sundried tomatoes). And Rocco Forte may one day attempt to incorporate the hall into his culinary empire (a restaurant to be named *Mezzo Forte* – to evoke hushed song rather than loud opera).

Seriously though, when reading those mouth-watering lists of pieces, you, the audience, should remember that what seems to have been conjured in a trice has been built with sweat and ears. Not that tears are far away either. If ever you see harassed solo pianists (or violinists, or cellists – we will come to singers later) with glazed and confused expressions on their faces, it is probably because their routine of practice and performance has been interrupted by urgent requests from their agents (or managements as it is now fashionable to call them) for next season's programmes. The heat is on to find a magic formula that will interest the Wigmore and, afterwards, the summer festivals. There is so much music to choose from and, in order to stand out from the crowd, one has to make that choice cleverly. There are some artists who seem to be in the forefront of discovery and innovation, and this places pressure on their peers. (How many cellists live in daily fear of Steven Isserlis discovering yet another forgotten masterpiece?) One possibility is to recycle material played for a long time; another is to learn new things from scratch –

easier for the young than the old. A frequent solution, an energy-saving compromise, is to give the illusion of something new – old ideas given a facelift, which sometimes means pouring old wine into equally old bottles, with merely a change of label. A certain singer was famous for making up wonderful titles for various Schubert festivals around the world which, at the end of the day, simply amounted to further performances of his *Winterreise*.

Long ago it was enough to arrange a succession of pieces in chronological order and hope for the best. But now there has to be a more appetising approach than this – something the publicists would call a *gimmick* or an *angle*. During my visits to New York in the eighties I noticed these people would promote recitals only if there was a *series*, a cult long since transplanted here and growing with such fecundity that 'Ceres' would be more appropriate (Schubert wrote a long song about this mythological figure). If more than one concert is too expensive, perhaps the solution is to commission a *new work*. (This is often a last minute, and rather desperate, suggestion that is usually mooted too late for any serious composer to be able to comply with the request.) Most of the publicity gurus have not the slightest idea of what hard work programme building entails; all they know is that they need the 'copy' long before the artist has had a chance to learn the pieces, and that the sequence of events must look good (whether it sounds good is sufficient unto the day). One can only hope that the omnipotent editors of the arts pages will find a *tie-in* for a *piece*. All of this pressure results in a lot of ill-considered information going to press far too soon, and with insufficient thought and preparation.

In these days, people who give the musical infantry its marching orders from above know less and less about the nitty-gritty. It was not always so. There are fascinating letters, recently published, between the impresario Walter Legge and Furtwängler and Karajan; in these, suggestions are thrown back and forth concerning programmes for symphony concerts, and Legge demonstrates that he knows as much, if not more, about building programmes than the great conductors. The issues discussed are here to do with balance and contrast – not too much slow music, not too much levity, no juxtapositions which kill the effect of the two pieces when put together. The search is for the correct mix where each piece will shine in conjunction with its neighbours.

Those enamoured of orchestral concerts scour the advertised list (four or five pieces at most, usually less if whole symphonies are being performed) and respond favourably to the menu – 'I fancy going to that!' But it is the responsibility of the planners to ensure that the programme must somehow be more than the sum of its parts, and the verdict on that will be passed only at the end of the concert. This applies to song recitals as well, but in comparison to the large building-blocks of sound in symphony concerts, or even the group of sonatas proposed by the violinist or cellist, the making of a song recital is a Swiss watchmaker's task where a large number of small and intricate moving parts have to be co-ordinated. A single symphony can last an hour or two, but a song, including some of the most potent of them, can last less than two minutes. The making of a recital programme is like the laying of a multi-coloured mosaic where each song, or part of a song, is only a tiny coloured chip, a small part of the overall pattern. Song recitals are therefore more of a nuisance to plan than any other, and concert managers and agents hate all the work that they entail, above all because of the cost in time and energy of preparing the printed programme.

The management of the Wigmore Hall have thought about this problem long and hard; the result is that their programme books (put together by the Hall's Paula Best, and the designer Peter Williamson) are quite simply the best to be found anywhere on the song recital circuit, both in terms of accuracy and information. (The work of Richard Stokes in terms of programme notes is astonishingly prolific.) But apart from an out of tune singer and incompetent accompanist, there is no area of the song recital where there is greater scope for mishap and disappointment than the programme book. It may be interesting for a moment to step outside the hallowed portals of the Wigmore Hall, and glimpse the problem in less lofty surroundings. Imagine that you are the secretary of a small concert club in the provinces that has invited a singer to give a recital (a rare enough occurrence, goodness knows, in these days, probably for the reasons outlined below). A year before the event all your urgent requests for further details will almost routinely be ignored by the agents, too busy with other more important matters to reply immediately. You simply have to be patient to discover or receive (a) the name of the accompanist (this decision is in the hands of the invited singer who may not be certain with whom she will be happy to work in a year's time); (b) the list of songs (you will at least have a list of composers for your preliminary publicity, and even these are liable to change); (c) biographies of both singers and accompanist as well as photographs. When these things arrive with little time to spare for the hard-pressed local printer your work is only beginning. At last you know what the songs are, but unless the agents have been very kind and efficient you will be confronted with a bare list of titles, mostly in foreign languages.

There is some disagreement about what it is best to do next. Of course, the easiest option is simply to print the titles and hope for the best; perhaps the singer (or the accompanist, usually an obliging type) will speak for a few moments to introduce the songs and tell us what they are about. In actual fact this is a deadly solution. Although many people will say, 'We do love to hear the artists talking,' there is nothing that more easily kills the musical expression of the poem's essence than a verbal résumé, delivered from the platform, of the poem one is about to hear in a musical form. (A word of warning here to those who are tempted to stand in front of a Wigmore Hall audience and tell them, for example, that 'Reynaldo Hahn was a very famous French composer'. There is no concert hall in the world where it is less necessary, and less welcome, to patronise an immensely knowledgeable audience. If something is to be spoken from the stage it has to be carefully prepared for the sort of sophisticated ears that one finds nowhere else.)

In any case, an epigrammatic and elusive song sometimes needs more time to explain than to sing, the moment of magic is past before it has begun. If a song is a happy one, an upbeat introduction gives away the joke too soon, and a sad song, introduced in suitably grave tones, milks pathos dry to the least effect. Most performing artists are not as good at speaking spontaneously from the stage as they think they are; as they ramble on, the thread of sheerly musical drama, the tension which should build up as the recital progresses, is broken. The Songmakers' Almanac, it is true, specialises in readings between songs, but the poem about to be heard in a musical form is never explained, as such; the spoken material is always from another source, and it leads into that song without announcing it. The audience, hopefully curious about the juxtaposition, consults the printed programme to read the lyrics. In this way connections are made between the spoken literature in the home language, and the sung words in a foreign one. Indeed, a Songmakers' Almanac programme without the printed programme containing all the translations would be unthinkable. Speaking from the stage is never meant to be a short-cut substitute for the real key to the proceedings which should be at the audience's fingertips, and easily accessible to the eye.

Of course there is always the compromise of the song synopsis. The trouble with this solution favoured by some – a few printed words making a précis of the poem which the listener can quickly take in before the performance – is that most song texts reduced to the brevity of this sort of summation sound banal and even uneventful. The sound of a foreign language is built into the music; it is the language of the poet which has given rise to the musical shapes and contours of the song. At one time it was considered desirable to have singing translations, and many people have laboured many hours to fit English words to musical notes originally written to the rhythms of another language. This practise has all but died away, and in any case the artistic cost of this is too high to pay. Even if we understand (more or less) what the song is about, we have lost its artistic essence. It is the equivalent of soundtrack dubbing in the cinema which is irritating enough even in straightforward narrative movies; such translations cannot possibly capture the crucial relationship between magically fused word and tone. Surely it is the specific *manner* of saying 'I love you' that is moving, and not merely the bald fact that the sentiment is delivered in the *lingua franca*. The magic, brief and elusive, depends on the original language. The English-speaking audience has to understand at a glance what a foreign word or phrase means, at the very moment that it hangs in the air, at the very moment it comes off the singer's lips. As the listener hears the singer colour a particular German/French/Russian word with relish in the midst of a telling musical phrase, the curious listener should ask: 'Why that colour here?' And only a parallel bilingual translation is able to provide the answer.

Surtitles, spun out line by line in the opera house, would be far too expensive and distracting at the Wigmore; and they do not allow the listener to see the shape and contour of a poem at a glance. Given a practised recital-attending eye, sound and meaning are conjoined by a glance at the programme, and in an imperfect world where we do not all speak every language, this remains the best solution. Of course there is the danger that some members of the audience will be buried, head-down, in their programmes during the recital (and sometimes a less than magnetising perform-ance on stage is the cause of this inattention). But after a number of visits to the Hall, as the reper-toire becomes more familiar, most people learn to divide their attention between the performers giving the concert in front of them, and what is happening between words and music.

Despite many an attempt to short-cut the process and short-change the listener (singers sometimes fear that full texts divert the attention away from them, whereas they actually marshal the concentration), there is a long tradition of scrupulously

Pages from a programme book for a Hugo Wolf recital accompanied by the composer in Graz in 1893

prepared printed programmes that goes back to the times of the great song composers themselves. At the Wigmore Hall's Lieder recitals we are used to seeing the poems lined up in two columns – original text and cor-responding translation. In Germany a whole evening of Lieder in the home language of the audience is almost always graced with a programme book with full texts. (At the Wigmore Hall, an English song recital has the poems printed in the same way.) This is because a song is first and fore-most a poem (and often a great one in its own right) which has been set to music. One *sees* and *reads* a song as well as hearing it. This is part of the overall experience. The verbal imagery burns its way into the brain: reading the poem in black and white, at the same time as hearing the music which has brought that poem to life, is the way that a song stays

8

Verborgenheit.

Ed. Mörike.

Laß, o Welt, o laß mich sein!
Locket nicht mit Liebesgaben,
Laßt dies Herz alleine haben,
Seine Wonne, seine Pein!

Was ich traure, weiß ich nicht,
Es ist unbekanntes Wehe;
Immerdar durch Thränen sehe
Ich der Sonne liebes Licht.

Oft bin ich mir kaum bewußt,
Und die helle Freude zücket
Durch die Schwere, so mich drücket
Wonniglich in meiner Brust.

Laß, o Welt, o laß mich sein!
Locket nicht mit Liebesgaben,
Laßt dies Herz alleine haben,
Seine Wonnen, seine Pein!

Er ist's.

Ed. Mörike.

Frühling läßt sein blaues Band
Wieder flattern durch die Lüfte;
Süße, wohlbekannte Düfte
Streifen ahnungsvoll das Land.

Veilchen träumen schon,
Wollen balde kommen.
Horch, von fern, ein leiser Harfenton!
Frühling, ja du bist's!
Dich hab' ich vernommen!
Ja, du bist's!

9

Der Soldat.

J. v. Eichendorff.

Ist auch schmuck nicht mein Rößlein
So ist's doch recht klug,
Trägt im Finstern zu 'nem Schlößlein
Mich rasch noch genug.

Ist das Schloß auch nicht prächtig,
Zum Garten aus der Thür'
Tritt ein Mädchen doch allnächtig
Dort freundlich herfür.

Und ist auch die Kleine
Nicht die Schönst' auf der Welt,
So gibt's doch just Keine,
Die mir besser gefällt.

Und spricht sie vom Freien,
So schwing' ich mich auf mein Roß —
Ich bleibe im Freien,
Und sie auf dem Schloß.

with you forever. So if we care about this music, we have to make sure that the words, and what they mean, are available to the audience.

All this is a lot of extra work that has stupefied, and continues to stupefy, concert promoters who are not used to the medium. Outside the Wigmore Hall the frequently encountered attitude is 'All this work is not necessary with piano recitals, for heaven's sake! And it's so many pages of foreign-language-gobble-de-gook.' 'Can't be bothered with that!' is the underlying feeling, and then the organisations involved wonder why the concert in question fails to engage the audience! With a singer it is impossible to shut your eyes and allow the music to waft over you. Having been persuaded to provide the texts (perhaps at the artists' insistence) the less experienced promoter wanders innocently into a minefield of difficulty. One has to find translations, or commission them (apart from internet searches, there are some useful books in this line – *The Fischer-Dieskau*

Book of Lieder for example, and the recently published *A French Song Companion* – but they never contain everything). And then there are all the pitfalls which regularly waylay even the most well-meaning promoter. On reading the title *Frühlingslied* (Spring Song) by Mendelssohn most hard-pressed people, struggling against the printing deadlines, would be relieved to come across a translation, any translation, fitting those two search categories. But they have to be careful which *Frühlingslied* by Mendelssohn is meant: op. 8 no. 6 with a text by Friederike Robert? op. 19 no. 1 (Ulrich von Lichtenstein)? op. 34 no. 3 (Carl Klingemann)? op. 47 no. 3 (Lenau)? op. 71 no. 2 (Klingemann again)? Or the *Altdeutsches Frühlingslied* op. 86 no. 6, which happens to be Mendelssohn's last song? Of these, the third and fourth would be the most likely to appear in recital programmes, but one would need to check the first line of the poem to make sure.

There is no quick way of learning about the song repertoire. One may as well suggest a short-cut to reading Japanese. You either know all those different characters or you don't. Each poem is about something different, even if the poet is a familiar figure (how many English-speakers would know about Goethe, for example, if it were not for the musical connection?). Every song has a pair of parents – composer and poet, and each of these brings with them a rich tapestry of background and an ever-widening circle of allusions. Throw a stone into the water and watch the ripples multiply – this is what happens when you hear a song: there is the beauty of the music itself (thanks to the composer) and the wisdom of the words (thanks to the poet) and the allure of the voice and the humanity and intelligence behind it (thanks to the singer) and the illustrative felicities of the accompaniment (yes, it is true the accompanist does not mind if he is also noticed). The composer has a story which has affected the composition of that song, but the poet too has quite a different story (sometimes many years, or even centuries, before the music was created). Thus each song has a twin existence: as an example of the composer's craft, and as a literary entity, perhaps raised to a higher expressive power by the music, but still very much the product of a literary mind.

So far we have only talked about the difficulties of making the programme book. But someone has to assemble those titles into an order. That is, technically speaking, the singer's job; but it is a task which often falls to the accompanist, simply because he has the experience and aptitude. His whole working life is devoted to gaining an overview of the song repertoire. His singers are occupied in other fields – opera, oratorio, concert work with orchestra. They tend to know the music suitable for themselves, but seldom have a working knowledge of the larger picture (there are honourable exceptions, of course). Because the accompanist has played for other people, because he has heard and played repertoire with one singer which may be equally suitable for another, one of his jobs, prime minister to the monarchs of song, is to advise and warn on matters of repertoire.

A whole book could be written on this subject, but audiences might be interested to read some of the things that go through this accompanist's head when planning a song recital. Here are some of the separate elements of this perplexing Rubik's Cube, all of which have to be made to line up convincingly at the end:

Composers: One has to decide whether the evening is given over to a celebration of one composer, a pair of them (usually one in each half), or a whole sequence of names – perhaps a different composer for each of up to six groups (a maximum of three in each half). If there are more than six names it is better to make a feature of the bewildering variety and plan a recital with a different composer for every song. In a number of Songmakers' Almanac programmes the composer himself was the basis for a 'song biography' following the course of a life (Haydn, Mozart, Beethoven, Schubert, Mendelssohn, Schumann, Wolf, Fauré, Mussorgsky, Poulenc, Britten and so on). In the case of Mozart and Duparc we were able to offer the complete works for voice and piano in a single evening.

Poets: Usually a secondary consideration, but a useful means of creating unity out of diversity in assorted groups. For example, one can either have a group of Armand Silvestre settings by Fauré, or use Silvestre's poetry as a thread with which to string together settings by (also for example) Boulanger, Chabrier, Chaminade, Chausson, Duparc, Lalo, Massenet and so on. Occasionally the poet is the pivotal figure of the programme, as in the recent Goethe series at the Wigmore, or in Songmakers' Almanac programmes about Verlaine, Mörike, Byron, Pushkin and Shakespeare – the binding thread of the celebration I devised for sixteen singers for the reopening of the Wigmore Hall in 1992.

Performers: Occasionally great artists have been the subject of pro-

Peter Pears

grammes. I invented the name 'Songmakers' Almanac' because my definition of those who make songs includes composers, poets *and* performers, and this coinage encompasses them all. We devoted programmes to Johann Michael Vogl (Schubert's first singer) and Maggie Teyte, as well as celebrations in honour of such contemporary artists as Gerald Moore, Peter Pears, Hugues Cuenod, and Eric Sams (the last two still very much with us). A singer like John McCormack has often been the subject of lighter programmes which feature the ballads he sang inimitably, and recently at the Wigmore Dawn Upshaw presented a programme in homage to the important French soprano Jane Bathori.

Other themes: These can take over an entire concert, or different parts of it, and the possibilities are limitless, almost always deriving from the poetry, and its subject matter (such as nature, flowers, childhood, lullabies, serenades, birds, animals, different countries and so on). Chronology is also a very important theme – thus songs from a particular year or epoch can be grouped together in all their variety. Songmakers' Almanac offered an 1888 programme, a First World War programme, as well as a decade-by-decade celebration of the twentieth century, a theme taken up years later by Simon Rattle for an orchestral series. We also presented programmes devoted to the months of January and December where the course of the evening's music was dictated by the various anniversaries which occured on the 31 days of those months.

The singer: Despite the fashion for creative devising, it is not necessary to have a thematic recital on every occasion. On the contrary, it is something of a relief to return to the simplicities of the conventional format, especially when the performer concerned is a big personality. In most celebrity recitals the theme is the singer himself, or herself – the binding thread being his or her view of the world through music. Here it is the strength of the artistic personality offered to us that unites various composers and styles into a cohesive evening's entertainment. However, even in the case of a recital planned in an utterly conventional manner, certain important things have to be taken into account.

Contrast and variety: Here the challenge is to keep the attention of the public. Too many light-hearted songs in the programme and we have been, as Jane Austen remarked, 'delighted long enough' – the whole evening seems to have consisted of insubstantial desserts. Too much meat and potatoes can be equally tiring – this is something that only the very greatest artists can get away with although, when they do, one emerges from the Wigmore deeply moved and improved, as if after *Parsifal*. Performers should not count on this reaction, however; all too often their own musical earnestness and proselytising fail to carry the audience with them. Moods should vary, length of songs should vary, the tempo of songs should vary and above all (this is one of the most important hidden secrets) the keys in which the songs are sung should be arranged in a very careful sequence. This is truly a creative side of recital planning which momentarily lifts the anthologist's task of binding together garlands of other men's flowers (as first Montaigne, and then General Wavell, put it) into that of a composer, or at least musical arranger. The juxtaposition of two songs in the same keys makes for dullness, and the tonal subtlety by which two items are linked can suggest everything from a delicious *segue* where one song slides into another, to a sudden and brutal change of mood brought about by a type of tonal dislocation. This care about all the tonal implications of programming is even more important when planning a sequence of songs for a disc.

These summaries only scratch the surface of what is required to make a good programme. Many an evening can more or less obey all these rules and still fail to come to life. There has to be an added element of spark which can only equate with a theatrical feel, something built into the sequence by its creator which promotes a feeling of denouement whereby the audience will be increasingly engaged with the music. An added complication is the shared recital involving more than one singer, where each artist has to be kept 'in play' and the repertoire has to be heard to be evenly divided between them in terms of length and efficacy. And once speech and movement begin on stage, the skills of a stage director (or a bossy accompanist) are needed to make things run smoothly. Too little liveliness is boring, but a moment of dance, though tempting, is dangerous: it crosses the threshold of what is acceptable on a concert hall stage, and takes the evening into the realm of a 'show' which can never be properly developed in a recital room like the Wigmore. The all-singing, dancing *Die schöne Müllerin* (suggested title *The Show in a Million* with 'Riverdance') probably awaits us, but not, thank heavens, at the Wigmore. Not until we get a revolving stage at least.

A well-made programme, like a well-made poetry anthology, is a work of art in its own right. Both presuppose an enormous overall knowledge from which the chosen works are selected. (One has only to look at the famous *Love* anthology of Walter de la Mare to feel humbled by the vast range of his literary sources and his mastery of them.) The tendency these days is for the titles of promised events to be much more interesting than the actual content of the programme which is delivered on the day. It is the title, packaging of a kind, which seems to be the most important thing for the publicity, and once tickets are sold it is unlikely that failure to deliver all that has been promised will result in a mass walk-out. For example, if one were to decide in advance (without prior research) to put on a concert entitled *Composers and Painters*, one might confidently expect to find a vast wealth of song material to draw on. In fact this is not the case, and such a programme would require a great deal of ingenuity and out-of-the way knowledge to make it work. Like that perpetually recurring and re-labelled *Winterreise* (a work where Schubert does our programme planning for us) we would almost certainly find the same old Granados and Poulenc that come to everyone's mind. Finding other new items would be difficult enough, and then, as I have already pointed out, they have to be placed in an order which seems fun, illuminating, inevitable, simply *right*.

Every recital is in its own way a version of *Pictures at an Exhibition*. A painter is honoured with a retrospective every so often – and then it is obviously very important how his works are hung, and in what order. (Much of the time he will be content to allow his works to be bought one at a time, each piece finding its home in a different place.) But for a musical performer, the sequence in which his or her wares are displayed is of the utmost importance. We are always searching for the secret formula which allows our various skills, and those of our colleagues, to be heard to the best advantage in the course of a single evening. The amount of thought that has gone into many an evening at the Wigmore Hall is often amazing, especially considering that it is all over in a single evening – something conceived for the Hall and nowhere else. It is a measure of the affection for, and awe of, the Wigmore's reputation and its audiences that many of us in the music business have spent countless hours concocting what we hope will be delectable bills-of-fare, quickly consumed and gone forever. But the success of many years of high standards in this area have resulted in accolades from around the world. As a result it is difficult to find a seat at the Wigmore, much less a table, and the 'maître d', the incomparable Bill, is one of the most courted and respected men in town whom no-one can bribe for a reservation. And as for our stars, we display them where they really matter, neither at the door, nor in the Michelin guide, but on stage where they appear nightly, sometimes more than three at a time.

The Friends Speak

Editor's note: The Friends of Wigmore Hall were invited to contribute personal memories for inclusion in this book. As always with the Friends, the response was immediate and generous. For reasons of space it has not been possible to include every contribution received but all of them will be added to the Hall's valuable collection of archive material. In some cases the contributions which follow have been edited for length.

A visit to the Wigmore Hall provides a unique pleasure. It is, of course, memorable for its music. But going to the Wigmore is not just a musical event. It is a considerable experience in itself. And one of the great features of that experience is the audience.

The Wigmore audience has a special characteristic, unlike any other. There is, it might be said, a kind of Wigmore person. Enthused, garrulous (or, at least, let's say talkative), involved, with an endless host of friends, and apparently – as far as music is concerned – all-knowing. Wigmore people seem to be a kind of extended family, spotting each other with whoops of delight as the audience piles into the foyer. It grows into an ever-widening circle of greetings, hellos and exchanges of news. An evening at the Wigmore is almost as much a social happening as a musical.

I could swear there is a kind of Wigmore person look. When we go to other venues (which we try to do as seldom as possible. Why suffer?) it is quite amusing to try to spot the Wigmorites who might be present. You can tell them at a distance, can't you? It's a particular kind of liveliness, excitability, a gleam in the eyes, a waving of the arms, an air of passionate anticipation. A sort of relish. But it is the knowingness of the Wigmore person which is the most formidable. They really know their music. And their performers. It underlies their rapt identification with each performance – and for the uninitiated can be quite daunting.

Take the following episode, which occurred one evening during a well-known Wigmore tradition, the Ceremony of the Cloakroom Queue. At the end of the recital the performer will usually finish with a climactic encore. Unless you miss this culminating act, you find yourself afterwards bolting for the cloakroom, along with the rest of the audience. And unless you are seated at the back, chances are that you come to rest on the staircase, having pushed women and children to one side in vain. This staircase wait, which can be quite extensive, is an occasion to exchange views and impressions. It even takes on a life of its own.

On that particular evening, the pianist had concluded with a charming piece which was lilting and full of spirit but which he had unfortunately not announced. As the Cloakroom Queue settled down for a nice long rest, the following exchange took place.

Man behind me to his companion: 'That was a lovely encore. I wonder what it was?'

His lady friend: 'I'm not quite sure.'

Voice at the bottom of the stairs: 'It's Schubert.'

Voice halfway to the top: 'Moments Musicaux.'

Voice nearer the bottom: 'Number Three.'

Voice just in front of me: 'In F minor.'

And quite naturally, it was. It's worth coming to the Wigmore, just to get into the Cloakroom Queue.

A. D. FARBEY

In 1947, when I was nine, my parents decided that I would benefit from a boarding-school education, and accordingly packed me off to a preparatory school in north-west London. On the staff, along with 'ex-Army boxing champion' and other demobbed academics, the Director of Music (although I'm sure there was no such title) was a Maurice Lanyon. He had, I think, been in the RAF, but he was, in some way which schoolboys only sense, different from the other staff. In fact, I think that he simply cared about teaching, and was disappointed when we failed to meet his standards. He trained the chapel choir, taught us the piano, but was most feared as a teacher of Latin: his wrath when faced with shoddy 'prep' was frightening.

In those days, there were seldom any trips away from school. We could apply for *exeats* to go to the local shops, but as we had no pocket money, we soon discovered that pinching (rationed) bars of chocolate was too risky. Most prized, therefore, were summons (not really invitations) to go to concerts at the Wigmore Hall. On weekend afternoons, organised sport at school permitting, Mr Lanyon would take three of his pupils out of school to piano recitals. In our school blazers, we would travel by bus and Northern Line into London. When we got to the Wigmore Hall, we were fascinated by the uniformed doorkeeper who would step out from the covered entrance, with umbrella if raining, to open taxi doors. Inside, we always hoped to have seats on the keyboard side, and towards the front; but (as now), I always seemed to be sitting in the middle of the hall, and behind a very large head. Often, ladies would wear a hat, which made for an additional obstacle for a small boy.

Looking back over fifty years, the music we heard always seems to have been Chopin. I can't believe that everyone played all-Chopin recitals but I have absolutely no recollection of anything else. Who did we hear? We never had programmes but on arriving at the Hall, we swept down the racks of leaflets to take back to school. Jan Smeterlin, Malcuzynski, Moiseiwitsch, Weingarten, Mewton-Wood and Kendall Taylor (they can't have been so good because they were obviously English) were, I'm fairly sure, amongst those we heard. I think Gieseking, Magaloff, and the even then not very youthful Shura Cherkassky were there. As to whether they were any good I haven't the slightest idea. It would be lovely to say: 'Even at the age of eleven, I realised that the playing of X was something I would treasure for the rest of my life.' But the only criteria I could apply was whether they played loud and fast. Anyone who played the 'Funeral March' Sonata or the op. 53 Polonaise was popular. No doubt the finer points of performance passed us by, but a fistful of wrong notes would have us digging each other in the ribs. I do recall, though, that I asked my parents for a record of the Fantaisie-Impromptu for some birthday. I was given a record of José Iturbi which greatly disappointed me: I knew it didn't go like that, but who the pianist was who set my standard I have no idea.

Just occasionally, perhaps when Mr Lanyon was in a particularly good mood, and we had time to spare before going back to school, we would be taken through the doors at the front of the hall and into the Green Room to thank the pianist personally. Mr Lanyon headed our queue, shook the great man's hand, addressed a few words of gratitude in reverential tones and then introduced us as a group. We shuffled forward, orderly queuing being a boarding-school characteristic, each saying 'Thank you very much, sir,' and thrusting the programme leaflet forward for signature. We then rushed outside to study and compare the autograph. I never gave a thought about who paid for these outings, and at that age it certainly didn't occur to us that Mr Lanyon probably paid everything out of his meagre teacher's wage.

After I left school at thirteen, I never saw Mr Lanyon again. I went off to the main school where the only concerts were by visiting musicians. But those visits to the Wigmore Hall set me off on my love of music, and for that I have always been grateful. Although a martinet and stickler, Mr Lanyon never treated these concerts as part of the school syllabus. He didn't tell us who or what we were going to hear – there was no preparation at all. So these outings were just something to enjoy, like going to Lord's or Twickenham to watch the Varsity match. Fifty years on, my idea of heaven is a day at the Test Match, followed by a walk in the evening sun, down Baker Street and along Wigmore Street, to the Hall for an evening of Chopin. And as I listen, I look round about me to see if any short-trousered schoolboys are starting out on their own journey into music.

ANTHONY BRAMLEY-HARKER

Many others will write tributes to the Wigmore Hall, its legions of great artists, its uniquely attentive audiences, the incomparable William Lyne – I want to single out Graham Johnson. There is nobody living who has done more for song. Here is a pianist of astonishing sensibility who is also a great scholar, not only of music but of literature, with a depth and breadth of knowledge that is unequalled among musicians in my view. Furthermore, this isn't confined to his writing: his eloquence informs, is crystalline, witty, never patronising, when he speaks to the audience. The anthologies he devised for the Songmakers' Almanac were revolutionary when first performed, and the Wigmore is the Songmakers' home base. There's no place like it.

JILL BALCON

Alfred Brendel

The Lindsay Quartet

Horszowski spans the years: early and late photographs

Tatiana Nikolayeva

Going through my 1990s programmes has been fascinating, especially when one sees new discoveries rapidly becoming stars. Matthias Goerne's debut recital in 1994 with the *Schwanengesang*, for instance: he had been heralded as an 'outstanding new Lieder singer' by William Lyne who had heard him in Brussels. Even at this first appearance there was standing room only. And then his *Winterreise* with Alfred Brendel in May 1999! He had already given an awe-inspiring performance in January 1997 at which Brendel was present. Ian Bostridge has been another such. Until 1995 he was still a junior research fellow in Oxford, and when I saw him on the Wigmore platform in January 1996 he looked about fifteen. *The Times* critic said of that concert (Schubert and Britten) that it was 'some of the finest singing the Wigmore Hall has heard in the last ten years.' We heard him again that year, singing with Robin Blaze Britten's haunting setting of the Chester miracle play *Abraham and Isaac*, one of the works chosen by William Lyne for his October anniversary celebrations. Of rising young pianists I particularly remember Till Fellner's first Wigmore appearance in September 1995 with an all-Schubert programme. We travelled back 150 miles from Wales for that concert.

GILLIAN AVERY

We have been attending concerts at the Hall for close to 30 years and love it dearly. We remember well the days before the 1990s refurbishment – the meagre sustenance for the body (coffee urn, plastic beakers and cellophane-wrapped sandwiches) contrasting sharply with the rich repasts for the spirits. Very special memories include the magnificent string quartet cycle in 1987, when the Lindsays and other quartets played all the Haydn quartets; the occasional visits by Alfred Brendel (and how wonderful it is to see him in the audience as well as on the platform); the Shostakovich preludes and fugues played by Tatiana Nikolayeva in 1993; hearing the young Cecilia Bartoli in recital (especially the Rossini centenary recital) before she became even more famous; listening to the young Ian Bostridge as his career took off, and the maturity and insight he brings to all he sings; the fabulous voice of Jessye Norman in Strauss. Other memorable cycles include Schiff's Schubert recitals and, more recently, Angela Hewitt's Bach recitals and lectures.

There is so much to write about, but the greatest joy is that the Hall is there for us to enjoy. Long may it thrive and delight us.

CELIA & ROY PALMER

Mieczyslaw Horszowski's 1986 Wigmore Hall recital proved to be the first of four over the next five years. He had probably the longest career of any Western classical musician. Born on 23 June 1892, at seven he performed one of his compositions for Emperor Franz Josef; he played for Fauré, Saint-Saëns, Granados and Joachim, studied with Leschetizky and did concerts with Ravel, Casals and Toscanini; and when a child he met a lady who had studied with one of Mozart's sons.

Eighty years after his Wigmore Hall debut, on 5 June 1986 I saw him for the first time, a small man with a large head and white hair. He walked on, bowed and started to play: Bach Preludes and Fugues; Mozart's Fantasia K.397 seemed rather loud (he was deaf); Beethoven's *Pastoral* Sonata had a powerful virtuoso fourth movement, though he was totally devoid of ego or showy pyrotechnics. He hummed during the *Children's Corner Suite* of Debussy (whom he heard play); this included a rhythmic and humorous *Golliwog's Cakewalk*. Horszowski was famous for his Chopin: a grandly sombre Polonaise, op. 40/2, a massive climax to the op. 36 Impromptu, and the *Bolero*, of nimble virtuosity. After one encore and three more returns he received a standing ovation, as at each concert.

Dozens of people were queuing backstage, including Murray Perahia, who earlier spoke of Horszowski's 'wonderful' playing. Horszowski married for the first time aged 89! I suggested to his wife that he might want to sit down, but he was still standing when I left, despite saying he was suffering from jetlag and that Perahia 'was used to zooming about the world'. We shook hands, he signed my programme and I asked if he would be returning next year. He replied, 'I don't know if I'll be here.'

He was, on 11 June 1987: Bach/Liszt, Beethoven's Sonata 2 with more rubato than Schnabel, Schumann's *Träumerei* and Chopin: Polonaise no. 1, a shimmering Impromptu and Scherzo 2 in one span. There were two encores.

He seemed less sprightly on 21 June 1990: Bach, Beethoven, Schumann's *Papillons* with great delicacy, and a remarkable Chopin group: Nocturne, Impromptu, Waltz and Scherzo 1, whose two dissonant chords after the trio seemed to hang on the air. The encores were *Träumerei* and Chopin's Etude op. 25/2, Horszowski returning to a rapturous standing ovation. When I shook hands with him backstage, he said, 'I cannot see and cannot hear.'

There was a tremendous buzz of anticipation at Horszowski's last London concert on 4 June 1991 (aged almost 99). Playing often with eyes closed, Mozart's Sonata k.570 had a sublime slow movement; after Beethoven's *Tempest* Sonata and Schumann's *Arabeske*, Chopin: Mazurka, Nocturne, a fleet Etude op. 25/2 and the *Fantaisie-Impromptu* played with heart-easing simplicity. Two encores, including *Träumerei*, one return, and, although the ovation continued for three more minutes, he was gone forever.

He continued to teach, and died on 22 May 1993 aged 100. We shall not see his like again.

DAVID MOLDON

Our first concert was as recent as 17 September 1986. We had been disappointed not to succeed in the ballot for the WNO *Ring* at Covent Garden and something just had to be done. The holiday was over; autumn and winter stretched infinitely ahead. What spurred us to book this particular concert, we cannot now recall. A lady with a lovely face walked onto the platform. A pianist sat down and began Beethoven's *Mailied*. A whole new world began to open. By the time he and she came to 'O Erd, O Sonne, O Glück, O Lust', winter was once again behind us and a summer that will last for ever had begun. Our wonder grew and grew; a song about a violet by Mozart, a song by a composer called Schubert of whom we had heard but whose songs we did not know, a song by a composer called Loewe of whom we certainly had not heard and then at the end of the first half Loewe again and lastly Schubert again – *Gretchen am Spinnrade*. Imagine hearing this for the first time, without knowing or expecting, 'und ach sein Kuss'; the lady with the lovely face lost her years and became the 18-year-old Gretchen. Her name, of course, was Elly Ameling. She opened the door of the house and we are still exploring its rooms.

And then there was this strange man who entered the hall from the back, when everyone else was seated, who must, we thought, be her husband who looked after her. To us, William Lyne is always Mr Ameling.

Sir Andrew Longmore

Brigitte Fassbaender had a long and distinguished relationship with the Wigmore Hall as a magnificent singer so it was a joy to renew my acquaintance with her by attending her first series of master classes here in March 1996.

Here was ability and communication at its best. All of the ingredients needed were in place: a group of enthusiastic singers of mixed ability and experience, an interested and in many cases knowledgeable audience and a truly great singer/teacher. It was immediately obvious that Brigitte loved her profession, was eager to guide, assist, indeed, at times, to rescue her pupils. She had such a depth of talent and teaching skills that, with the lightest of touches, warmth, humour and seemingly infinite patience and integrity she was able to transform their performances in minutes! No trace of remoteness or arrogance: no desire to produce carbon copies of herself, just an honest and enthusiastic attempt to bring out the best in her pupils and encourage them to take a much deeper look at the meaning of what they were singing. (The declared intention was to help them with interpretation but inevitably she had to offer guidance about technique.) If one approach failed she tried another and one felt that, provided the singer had enough basic talent and desire to learn, the different possibilities and approaches needed to get them to the winning post were virtually infinite. But Fassbaender does not give in easily, it seems and she cares very much about nurturing young talent. A highly intelligent, sensitive, straightforward and likeable human being she is always on the singer's side – firm but positive and genuinely pleased for them when the penny dropped.

Should anyone have thought the first series of master classes might have been exceptionally good, perhaps even a 'one-off' they would have been wrong. Since then Brigitte has done it all again for us twice. Each has been every bit as enjoyable, useful and successful as the first. Thank goodness she clearly enjoys teaching, likes the Wigmore Hall and bless her heart, the audience as well so, with a little luck, we may continue to benefit from her presence in the future.

JOAN ROBINSON

A Liederabend consisting entirely of Hugo Wolf songs is special. Even more so is a Wolf evening devoted to settings of a single poet, and it was with particular pleasure that I heard the concert devoted to the poems of Mörike (4 October 1996).

The singers were Gerald Finley and Joan Rodgers, accompanied by Roger Vignoles. It was an evening of highly accomplished music making, but for me the enjoyment of the concert was greatly enhanced by the pre-concert talk.

Words and music seem to be fused together more closely in the songs of Wolf than in any other composer. It was therefore revealing to consider them separately. Richard Stokes gave us Eduard Mörike, the elusive lyric poet (and quiet country pastor). Roger Vignoles considered the Lieder from the accompanist's viewpoint, while Eric Sams contributed a comprehensive vision of Wolf's art. Reading his book on Wolf is an education in itself, but to listen to the man himself illuminating so many points of detail was a rare privilege.

The intimate atmosphere of the Bechstein Room created the impression that we were eavesdropping on a conversation between friends, who just happened to be experts in their field. It was an ideal preparation for the evening's concert.

CARL MURRAY

Coughing in the Wigmore Hall: This is not allowed. In every other concert hall in London you normally think you're sitting in a TB sanitorium, but not in Wigmore Street.

Scene: at the beginning of a concert with Graham Johnson and Olaf Bär, while Mr Johnson is still going through his pre-concert chat (with musical illustrations) I get a coughing fit. I try to stifle it as much as possible, but what I really need is a good run at clearing my throat. Mr Johnson's talk is finally drawing to a close and I'm just getting ready for a last quick hack, when the man in front of me turns around with a smile on his lips but raging murder in his eyes and asks: 'Would you like a sweet?'

How very English!

I thank him but decline the offer and use the cover of applause to get rid of the frog in my throat. Thereafter I manage to remain silent throughout the recital, no doubt much to everyone else's relief.

IRENE BOOGERMAN

My association with the Wigmore Hall (on both sides of the platform) goes back over sixty years. My very earliest memory is of taking part, before the war, at the age of seven, in a student concert put on by Tobias Matthay whose school of pianoforte playing was just around the corner in Wimpole Street. I was recruited along with a young cellist to provide a chamber music element amongst all the pianists and we played the Haydn G major trio.

After the war I took part in concerts with various chamber ensembles, the most poignant of which, in retrospect, was the debut in April 1957 of a small chamber ensemble which Dennis Brain formed the year before his death. Perhaps bored with the easy perfection of his own playing, Dennis was looking for new challenges and like so many other instrumentalists was attracted by the thought of conducting. He gathered together a small group of friends and colleagues to form the Dennis Brain Chamber Orchestra. That first concert was an all-Mozart programme, apart from a piece for oboe by Fricker in which his brother Leonard was the soloist. The critics, whilst praising Dennis's general musicianship, were politely lukewarm about his conducting; undeterred, he continued to devote a lot of energy to his new project and it was just beginning to get off the ground when he was killed in a car crash the following year.

The last time I played at the Wigmore Hall I remember for purely personal reasons. It was in the autumn of 1962 with Paul Tortelier who had also taken to the baton for that particular occasion. He was in Gallic mood and berated us (the ECO I think) for our lack of elegance. 'Think of the elegance of the countryside, not of the city,' he exhorted us. As I was about to leave the profession to marry and live in the depths of Devon, this remark struck home.

As a member of the audience I have to single out the debut of the Amadeus Quartet in April 1948, which was remarkable not just for the arrival of a brilliant young quartet on the scene, but for the whole sense of occasion which it generated. The influx of refugees from Hitler's Europe, which had so revitalised the musical scene in London, was nowhere more in evidence than here. A new audience had emerged which included a core of extremely knowledgeable and accomplished amateur musicians with exacting critical standards which conditioned musical life in London for several decades. At this concert there was almost a party atmosphere as well as a critically expectant mood. Not only had word got around about this talented young group; many people knew them personally and had possibly played chamber music with them in their own homes – probably in exchange for a square meal. Times were hard for young musicians then. The Mozart quartet was played with a Viennese charm not heard for some while in London, the Verdi quartet, not often played then, was new to many people, and they concluded with a robust performance of the Beethoven 3rd 'Rasoumovsky'. The critics were not as glowing as they might have been but the audience was in no doubt that we had witnessed the arrival of a major new ensemble. The rest, of course, is history.

I have left until last the concert which over these many decades has left the most enduring impression upon me. That was the first recital given over here (in 1947) by Dinu Lipatti. The luminosity of his playing and the directness of his entire personality defy description and I shall not attempt it. I only know that to this day (fifty years on) I still feel a lift of the spirit when I recall the event.

In a changing world the Wigmore Hall has been a thread of stability in my life as well as a constant source of pleasure.

ELIZABETH BOENDERS-OXENHAM

It was one of those tiny gestures which seem to say so much: in this case, 'Wait until I've sung through to the end of this group of songs,' 'Thank you but no thank you,' and (most clearly of all), 'The music will make more sense and have a greater impact if you respond to it in silence.' All of this Janet Baker communicated by standing completely still and raising her right hand (from the wrist only) by about 20 degrees, yet everyone saw it, took notice, and the precipitate clappers were immediately silenced. Without that gesture I myself might well have joined in the applause at that point; after all I was attending my first Lieder recital at the Royal Northern College of Music in October 1976. In the previous year (my first year at Manchester University and my first year living in a city) I had attended my first symphony concerts (at the Hallé); applause between movements was clearly not on. I had attended my first operas (ENO and WNO on tour) and applause after arias seemed to be expected. So which way should we respond to Schumann's *Frauenliebe und -leben* – movements or arias? I would definitely have joined in the applause if it hadn't been for that slight movement of the hand, but I might never have become the Lieder lover that I now am had I not been allowed to experience the full cumulative power of that song cycle on that evening.

We are a famously well-behaved audience, I read, the regular Lieder audience at the Wigmore Hall. It is October 1996, and I am now definitely a regular; at this point I probably average one WH song recital per week. 20 years on from Janet Baker in Manchester I know now how to behave. So when someone starts applauding Christoph Prégardien in the middle of his Schubert group, it is almost instinctual for me to wince. And yet. On this occasion I myself join in. Yes, I *will* applaud at this point. How else can I tell the performers that all their hard work (not just in preparation for this concert, but over a whole lifetime's training) *is* appreciated? Obviously Christoph Prégardien must know that his technical achievement and his interpretative understanding of *Du bist die Ruh* have

Elly Ameling

Elisabeth Schwarzkopf

Dinu Lipatti

just produced a performance that is as near perfect as can be imagined and that he is unlikely to equal again, but doesn't he have the right to know that the audience were paying attention? Not just generally. I can applaud at the end to say I have enjoyed the recital, but that isn't what I want to say. I want to clap *now*. I want to hold everything up to show some respect to the artists (and, as Janet Baker's motion of the hand reminds me) the composer and the poet. And so I break the rules; worse than beginning a sentence with 'and', I – a member of the Wigmore Hall Lieder audience – applaud after an individual song.

MALCOLM WREN

My attendances at the Hall go back some 50 years or more. In those far-off days the Hall was, of course, a venue for wonderful music making but it had about it a drab, dusty old-fashioned feeling and atmosphere. Presiding over the Ladies' Cloakroom was a dignified and elegant lady who wore a little black pill box hat perched on her head and a black dress with a frilly white pinafore. She sat at a small table and handed out cloakroom tickets – 1/- each. She would then hang your coat on one of the hooks provided. I never saw her stoop to wiping a lavatory seat or basin! She disappeared when the place was refurbished. In those days one just turned up for a concert and then went home. Now you feel you are among friends sharing a wonderful experience. The place has been transformed into a vibrant, friendly venue for music lovers, a kind of club of kindred spirits, and I cannot wait until the next concert. I have grown to love the place, a feeling which no other concert hall in London arouses.

BRONIA SNOW

Note from William Lyne: The cloakroom attendant was Viola (Vi) Gray, now in her nineties and still living just around the corner from the Hall. Her chair is still in 'the Ladies' in memory of Vi; we miss her. She still attends the Wigmore staff Christmas lunch.

When I was aged about seven in the early 30s my aunt took me to the Wigmore Hall to encourage me to continue playing the piano. Everyone was sitting comfortably in the auditorium and the pianist walked on – it was Arthur Rubinstein. He sat on the stool and there was absolute silence, until I said to my aunt in a loud voice, 'Who is that old man sitting up there?' 'Be quiet,' she whispered. Heads turned to see who it was. My aunt never forgave me for that little outburst.

JUNE DOIG

At a recital by Irina Arkhipova some time in the 80s a friend and I were sitting behind Elisabeth Schwarzkopf. In the interval my friend and I carried on about how wonderful Arkhipova was and Madame Schwarzkopf turned round to say she agreed entirely. I was moved to tell her of a night in Vienna in 1964 when she was singing the Marschallin and my then husband said to me after the performance, 'I wish I had a silver rose, I'd give it to Schwarzkopf.' She smiled with delight, kissed my cheek, and her eyes filled with tears. I've never forgotten it.

ILSA YARDLEY

Our most memorable concert was on 31 January 1997, the 200th anniversary of Schubert's birth. It was really a series of concerts, showing all the different aspects of Schubert's amazing genius. If only the composer himself could have heard it, he would surely have been deeply touched to know how well his music could be performed and appreciated. Could he possibly have imagined a performance of the G major Quartet like the one given by the Takács? We were brought up on the Amadeus, whose performance of this work seemed definitive, emphasising its moods changing from 'beautiful to frightening' in Norbert Brainin's words. Yet the Takács found a beauty and intensity that had us completely lost in the music, concentrating with no difficulty for the full 50 minutes.

Before the quartet, the piano and piano duet pieces had allowed a little light relief before culminating in the F minor Fantasy, endless melody

WIGMORE
HALL

Schubert Bicentenary Concert
Artistic Director: András Schiff

Friday 31 January 1997 at 6.00 pm
Sponsored by Risk Publications

András Schiff *piano*
Bruno Canino *piano*
Takács Quartet
Angelika Kirchschlager *mezzo soprano*
Christoph Prégardien *tenor*
Thomas Quasthoff *baritone*
BBC Singers *(male voices)*
Stephen Cleobury *conductor*
Radovan Vlatković *horn*
Garfield Jackson *viola*
David Waterman *cello*
Duncan McTier *double bass*

We regret that Cecilia Bartoli has cancelled her appearance
and we are very grateful to Angelika Kirchschlager who has
kindly agreed to sing an additional group of Schubert Lieder

PROGRAMME
Would patrons please stifle coughing as much as possible
and ensure that watch alarms are turned off
NB: MOBILE PHONES ARE BANNED FROM WIGMORE HALL

Franz Schubert (1797-1828)

6 Grand Marches for piano duet
No 1 in E flat major • No 2 in G minor • No 5 in E flat minor

4 Lieder
Auf der Bruck • Nachtstück • Nacht und Träume • Ganymed

Allegretto in C minor for piano

4 Lieder
Gretchen am Spinnrade • Wiegenlied
Der liebliche Stern • Die junge Nonne

Fantasy in F minor for piano duet

* * * * *

16 German Dances for piano

String Quartet in G major

* * * * *

Gesang der Geister über den Wassern

Auf dem Strom for tenor, horn and piano

6 Lieder
Der Wanderer • Der Zwerg • Der Tod und das Mädchen
Du bist die Ruh • Erlkönig • An die Musik

Nachthelle for tenor, male chorus and piano

Mondenschein • Liebe • Die Nacht for unaccompanied chorus

Ständchen for mezzo soprano, male chorus and piano

This recital is being broadcast live on BBC Radio 3 ◼

Cover painting of Schubert by Wilhelm August Rieder. © AKG London / Erich Lessing

1

The Schubert Bicentenary Concert programme

both beautiful and disturbing. Three solo singers gave contrasting songs and contrasting performances. Christoph Prégardien took all the 19th-century varnish off his songs, delivering them with purity and simplicity. Angelika Kirchschlager had a wonderful youthful freshness. But the language changed completely in the third part of the evening, 'prepared' by the G major Quartet. Thomas Quasthoff sung with a directness and passion that was almost overwhelming. His tremendous courage also came over, nowhere more so than in *Der Zwerg*, charged with a haunting beauty that is still fresh for us three years later.

It was hard to believe that there were still some more magic moments to come. *Nachthelle* and *Mondenschein* with their extraordinary high tenor parts touched the heavens while the low timbre of *Gesang der Geister über den Wassern* provided a most moving contrast. And it was a touch of genius to end with the beguiling *Ständchen*, sending us out just before midnight but with a spring in our step.

MARIE SACKIN AND SON PAUL

The Wigmore Hall entered my life early in 1944, a grim period, when it seemed as if the war would never end, there were quite a lot of bombing raids at night, succeeded, in June 1944, by the V1 'Doodle Bugs', flying bombs, that came over night and day in a steady stream and then the V2 rockets. In those days, the seats were of cast iron, minimally upholstered and most uncomfortable. From the apex of the cupola was suspended a light fitting, apparently by the flex, with a huge, red silk shade, which dangled just above the singer's head and I often used to wonder if, one day, it might not fall and what the effect would be. On several occasions, there were air raids during concerts, but I do not remember seeing any member of the audience leaving, nor any performer so much as bat an eyelid, a superb example of British phlegm.

There was always an atmosphere of excitement in the Hall, chiefly, I think, because no one would dream of going there unless they wanted to hear the music to be played. It had its eccentricities in those days, too. The box office was serviced by a man with only one hand, the other replaced by a hook, but he still managed to tear tickets out of the books then in use – at 10 shillings, 7/6 and 5 shillings (50p, 37.5p and 25p).

There were many exciting performances. Britten and Pears performed *Die schöne Müllerin*. Dennis Brain and Denis Matthews, both dressed as aircraftsmen in the RAF, played the Beethoven Horn Sonata. Later on, after the liberation of Paris, a number of French artists came over. The occasion that I remember best is the debut of Ginette Neveu, sharing a concert with Gérard Souzay, with Francis Poulenc playing the piano. Neveu was the greatest violinist I have ever heard, with a passion and power in her playing that I have never met in anyone else. It was a major tragedy that she was killed in an air crash a few years later.

Things got better in the spring of 1945 and then, suddenly, the war in Europe was over. Just after this, there was a memorable evening in the Hall, when a preview of *Peter Grimes* was given, a week before the first performance at Sadlers Wells and we heard, for the first time, that extraordinary music. Vaughan Williams, who was sitting a couple of rows in front of me, became so excited that he kicked his hat away and had great difficulty finding it at the end of the evening.

During the whole of that halcyon summer of 1945, with peace, at last, a reality, the Hall was very active and I was able to go there two, or sometimes three times a week, for chamber music and song of all sorts. Maggie Teyte sticks in the memory, as also does Gerald Moore, who was the predominant ensemble pianist, then and for many years afterwards.

D. J. I. GARSTIN

A concert hall is more than a space with particular architectural and acoustical properties. It has its own life and personality. Rationally, of course, it's only a matter of airborne vibrations within a given space, without need for subjective interpretation. But we know better.

In 1959-60 during the unrepeatable series of Lotte Lehmann's master classes, I still vividly remember a moment of absolute silence following Madame Lehmann's brief demonstration to the three young singers onstage of the phrase from the final Trio of *Der Rosenkavalier* – 'ich weiss' gar nichts, gar nichts.' I had never before heard that work, although

LOTTE
LEHMANN

in a series of

TWELVE
MASTER CLASSES

in
OPERA and LIEDER

Accompanist:
IVOR NEWTON

Management:
IBBS & TILLETT LTD., 124 WIGMORE STREET, LONDON, W.I

Lotte Lehmann's 1959-60 Master Classes

'Peter Grimes' Preview, 31 May 1945

Amadeus Quartet, 1953

WIGMORE HALL

BOOSEY & HAWKES
FOURTH   **CONCERTS**   SEASON

THURSDAY, MAY 31st, 1945, at 7 p.m.

Concert-Introduction to
PETER GRIMES

An Opera in three acts and a prologue
derived from the poem of George Crabbe
by Montagu Slater

Music by

Benjamin Britten

given by the producer and the principal
characters of the forthcoming production of

The Sadler's Wells Opera

on the 7th of June

Price 6d.

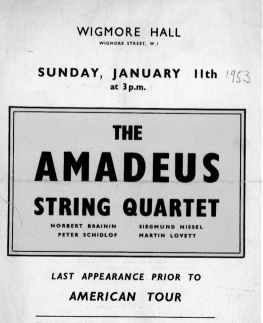

WIGMORE HALL
WIGMORE STREET, W.I

SUNDAY, JANUARY 11th 1953
at 3 p.m.

THE
AMADEUS
STRING QUARTET

NORBERT BRAININ   SIEGMUND NISSEL
PETER SCHIDLOF   MARTIN LOVETT

LAST APPEARANCE PRIOR TO
AMERICAN TOUR

TICKETS (including Tax): Reserved 9/-, 6/- Unres. 3/-
May be obtained at the BOX OFFICE WIGMORE HALL (Wel 2141) usual Agents and
IBBS & TILLETT LTD., 124 Wigmore Street, W.I
Ticket Office: WElbeck 8418   Hours: 10-5; Saturdays, 10-12
(for Programme P.T.O.)

many of the audience had, but we were all part of the deeply-felt silent moment of sheer emotion which greeted her short utterance – an inaudible lump in all throats and a missed beat of many hearts including mine, based on I knew not what. Unforgettable and still indescribable forty plus years on, and surely woven into the fabric of the Wigmore for all time.

Other moments easily recalled and deeply felt, include the nonagenarian Hugues Cuenod's hilarious rendering of 'Nous voulons une petite soeur', the wonder of the similarly aged Oda Slobodskaya's *sprechgesang* straight from the heart in the Songs of Gruszy, Elisabeth Söderström's enchanting mimicry of her own Swedish accent in commenting on a song, and Christa Ludwig's singing *Morgen* at her Wigmore Farewell Concert.

Recently, a talk by the architectural firm who originally designed the Hall ranged from the 19th century right up to the appropriate and not appropriate uses of computer technology. The warm buzz and friendly interest generated in the Bechstein Room on that occasion will also live on in the walls, even without a note of music being heard. All the shared tears and laughter, I believe, remain embedded in the air and the walls of the hall itself and can be retrieved by us as pleasure and nourishment for the heart during painful or happy times while remaining a living element of the Hall itself. The Education Department is now making it possible for children to become part of this lifelong alliance long before knowing why or how.

And that's why we come back to Wigmore Street yet again.

Jacqueline Faith

Wigmore Hall regulars are like the Three Bears – we expect to sit in 'our' seats . . . Long before we know names, we identify familiar faces as, say, A5 & 6 or U3 & 4 and get very confused – almost to the point of non-recognition – should they be transposed to B18 & 19 or V16 & 17.

There can be few other concert halls where one will receive an anxious phone call from a fellow regular to enquire after one's health, 'as we haven't seen you for the last two weeks.' And we have had our share of hospital visiting – and death.

Happily, more of us bump into each other at local recycling bins, in the food department of Marks & Spencer, even at other concert halls, theatres, museums, art galleries – though C7 is unlikely often to be found elsewhere since he claimed 246 concerts at Wigmore Hall in 1999 alone.

In November 1998 the front row regulars were invited to a party to celebrate the 90th birthday of A11 at which we were treated to a surprise concert – a surprise even to A11 – which turned out to be no less than an hour's recital by Sarah Walker and Roger Vignoles with every song chosen for its relevance to the birthday girl.

In September 1999 we celebrated the Golden Wedding of A7 & 8 culminating in a Wigmore Hall concert and party, preparations for which began more than six months earlier and which had to be kept secret from the wife. The husband asked me to liaise with the 14 other guests and him, an exercise even more complex than Falstaff's intrigues with the Merry Wives of Windsor. An added complication was that the guests had to keep our gift to the couple secret, and we were very grateful to the Wigmore Hall staff for generously aiding and abetting us in this!

Our next celebration is an 80th birthday party; not *quite* mine, though my very first Wigmore Hall concert was 47 years ago on Sunday, 11 January 1953 at 3.00 when the Amadeus Quartet played Haydn op. 74/1; Brahms op. 51/2 and Beethoven op. 59/2. Tickets cost 9/- (45p), 6/- (30p) and unreserved 3/- (15p). (I followed that at 7.30 with a jazz concert at the Gaumont State Cinema, Kilburn, featuring Cab Calloway.)

Having had the good fortune to have shared in nearly half of Wigmore Hall's life, I hope to have a few more years to continue to enjoy its civilised and civilising pleasures.

NINA DRUCKER (BB3)

Coda: And if dear BB3 did not know all of us *and* introduce us, we'd still be strangers. Recently, bumping into A14 (occasionally) on Eurostar a hectic chat on the lines of 'Why do we know each other so well' resolved itself into front row familiarity, was greeted by BB3 with incredulity as we had been introduced more than once!

A9 (not as often as I'd like).

During the forties I was a student at Queen's College in Harley Street, conveniently near Wigmore Hall where I began singing lessons with Miriam Lycette in one of the Hall's studios. I wish I could remember all the little stories she told me but one I can recall, which intrigued me especially, was the day her accompanist failed to attend her opera class. One of the staff, trying to be helpful, said that he happened to have a young man in the hall that morning who could sight-read anything, although he was only eighteen. Rather reluctantly Miriam asked him up to the studio only to be amazed at his immaculate playing of a very difficult Mozart score. It was her first meeting with Gerald Moore.

My piano teacher at Queen's was Mabel Floyd, a wonderful lady who also taught in Wigmore Studios, occasionally holding a pupils' concert in the Hall. I shall never forget one special evening, not just because I had some very difficult Liszt to play, but because of the clarinettist who ended the concert with the most beautiful performance of Schubert's *Shepherd on the Rock*. It was a very young Gervase de Peyer with his sister, Deidre, singing the soprano part.

I have never lived very far from Wigmore Hall and will always hold it in great esteem and affection.

Dorothy Foster

It always begins with a telephone call from Julia, who is the wonderfully efficient, funny, Co-ordinator of the Wigmore Hall Volunteer Friends. Would I be free on a date in the following few weeks to help stuff envelopes with a group of other Friends? 'Stuff' sometimes means labelling envelopes, and usually includes filling each with publicity for a forthcoming concert, education event, or music competition, and always means a lot of envelopes. But the session is always much more than that. It is the chance to hear news and views on artists and composers, swap ideas on subjects as diverse as the benefits of e-mail, meditation, and financial investments, also to learn a bit, or just gossip. I always hope I will be available. Refreshments are provided to maintain the momentum and various passing Wigmore Hall staff pop in to say hello. Best of all though is the knowledge that these sessions genuinely save costs for the Wigmore Hall, enabling more resources to go to seeking out the best in musical performance worldwide.

Alison Kidd

The reasons for my having such a soft spot for the Wigmore (for me it's not a Hall, it's more than that!) is that I made my concert debut there when I was a member of the Covent Garden Opera Company in the 50s, singing mostly Mozart and Richard Strauss. It was the conductor Peter Gellhorn who said to me, 'You must start singing Lieder.' And so together we started working on a concert programme which included, of course, Mozart and Schubert songs – but where to do them? Peter said, 'There's only one place – the Wigmore.' 'Goodness,' I said, 'will anyone come? I'm not a big name.' 'Well,' said Peter, 'we must get the critics in. Let's try to do a British première, a song cycle, for example. I'll try to find out what's not been performed here yet.'

The next morning Peter was on the phone. 'Adèle, the French composer Olivier Messiaen has written a wonderful song cycle, *Les Chants de Terre et de Ciel*, and it has never been sung here. If we could get Messiaen to come, just to play them for you, it would get the critics in . . .'

And so it was. Joan Ingpen, my agent, persuaded Messiaen to come; Peter accompanied the whole concert except for that one piece. The fact that the composer came all the way from Paris to play his songs for me meant we had an 80% house – and all the critics were there!

Adèle Leigh Enderl

In March 1956 I was married and went to live in a ground-floor flat in Earl's Court. Our landlord was an elderly white-haired man who lived in the basement flat together with about fifteen cats. Every evening as we returned from work we would meet our landlord, Mr Lake, walking to Earl's Court Station attired in evening dress. We were very curious as to what his evening jaunts entailed but never liked to ask. After some months I went one evening to attend a concert at the Wigmore Hall; to my amazement when the artists came on to the stage they were followed by Mr Lake, who was then, and had been for many years I believe, the resident page-turner for the Wigmore Hall.

JEAN MEIKLE

My first concert at the Wigmore in 1972 was not without its dangers; at that stage my knowledge of chamber music was close to zero.

As I emerged at its close I became conscious of a lingering presence: a diminutive female of considerable seniority wearing an elaborate full-length gown, decked out in jewellery – mainly jet – and wrapped rather precariously in a too generously proportioned fur stole. The ensemble was crowned by a pharaonic pile of gunmetal hair.

I sensed, correctly, that I was about to be addressed.

'You enjoyed the concert?' she challenged with an over-precise diction which betrayed her foreign origin.

Apprehensive of some deep conversation on the technicalities, I sought to register enthusiasm tempered by ignorance. 'I liked the Beethoven,' I proffered cheerily, 'though it's the first time I've heard it'.

I was scrutinised by startling, and startled, china blue eyes.

'You have never heard the Beethoven before?' she hissed.

I sensed a gaffe. Was this the most familiar work in the canon? Had she been at home with its melodies since, back in '96, Grandpapa dandled her on his knee in the conservatoire in Leipzig, Königsberg or Posen? Alternatively was there some strange house rule at the Wigmore that chaps could not simply wander in off the street unschooled and listen to advertised pieces?

I tried to rescue myself.

'Well, when I say never before . . . I mean, I do have the record.' This was untrue but seemed a pretty safe remark; she was hardly likely to demand the receipt from HMV.

The eyes lost none of their penetration.

'You have a *record* of the Beethoven?' she said with a conspiratorial glance at the backs of the departing audience. I felt as if I had admitted possession of the Maltese Falcon.

My panic grew. Perhaps the piece was not very famous but, *au contraire*, very obscure, unearthed from some dusty Viennese attic only weeks before by a zealous musicologist. This hardly seemed likely. Wherein, then, lay my transgression? Was the Wigmore so devoted to live performance that its denizens were sworn never to sully their ears with mere reproduction?

At this point my bestoled interrogator was joined by her friend, a taller and stouter woman also in full fig. They moved in line abreast towards the exit, seemingly on castors; there was nothing so vulgar as limb movements beneath all that heavy silk. The diminuendo was a recitation by the lesser to the greater.

'This young man has never heard the Beethoven, but he has a record . . .'

The stouter woman glanced back sharply at the sheepish figure in the crumpled suit, transfixed by this rehearsal of his previous convictions.

DAVID PETCH

We know how highly silence is prized at Wigmore Hall. Mobile phones are properly consigned to outer darkness, while a merely passive absence of noise has never been this audience's style. The quality of listening bears out what I've always suspected: that people really can *forget* to cough. Those who remember tend to be treated to glares that kill.

The uncanny thing, though, is the way that the very fabric of the building seems, like some benevolent ghost, to encourage this active silence whatever the time of day. One morning some months ago, early for an appointment, I sat in the deserted foyer near the foot of the stairs. The London traffic seemed very distant; brass rails were being polished in the empty hall; a solitary lad sat reading in the box office which was yet to open. There were no musicians rehearsing and, of course, there was no music jabbering from any radio, CD player or monitor. The contented spirit of the hall would rightly have been affronted.

After a concert, too, the place will often seem to re-assert its silent self. New to London at the beginning of the eighties, I'd been thrown into a state of emotional disrepair by the Fitzwilliam Quartet's account of the

Grosse Fuge, reaching Bond Street underground before realising that I'd left a bag under my seat. Returning, I found a silence in the now-empty, partly gaslit hall so deep that it might have possessed its own will, the very walls and chairs seeming to have absorbed the energy of the music which had ended just twenty minutes earlier.

ANDREW KEENER

We have many fond memories of the Wigmore Hall having attended concerts regularly there for the past 35 years up until our temporary move to Switzerland. These include Bill Lyne dashing backstage two minutes before the scheduled start of an important concert with a worried expression on his face to return triumphantly smiling to retake his seat with a word of explanation to the person sitting on his right. The loyalty of the staff and their longevity of service – the old front-of-the-house manager who only left the Hall's employ in 1998, and the various musicians who help fill the gaps in the box office waiting for their big break. The music students from Trinity are also a wonderful fixture on stage for piano recitals or accompaniment but their appearance seems to be getting rarer as more and more pianists learn the score by heart. Our favourite pianist is András Schiff who arranged the Schubert Anniversary concert.

It was not surprising that such a great pianist as András Schiff, very familiar with the places where Schubert lived and performed, should summon a coterie of German and Austro-Hungarians to help him celebrate the composer's anniversary. After a stunning concert, we went backstage and I presented him with a small book on the life of Schubert, published in London in the mid-nineteenth century. He was at first reluctant to accept the book, but when pressed, clutched it to his heart and for the rest of the evening was not parted from it. It was almost as if it he was carrying the score of a great and as yet undiscovered Schubertian work with him.

By carrying the book in the way a lecturer would carry his notes on his walk to the lecture hall at a university, he seemed to be indicating that he indeed did understand the secrets of how Schubert's music should be played and was delighted to be able to share them with whoever would listen. How true that was that evening, not just in his playing of Schubert pieces but also by the choice of the musicians he brought with him who further illuminated the brilliance of the composer.

Another wonderful evening consisted of a surprise encore from Anne Sofie von Otter, who after some Wolf songs sang two extracts from Hilaire Belloc's *Cautionary Tales*, set to music by Liza Lehmann. The songs included 'Jim', who ran away from his nurse and was eaten by a lion, and 'Matilda' who told lies and was burned to death. She sang them with such beautiful phrasing, frequently leaning forward to confide in us the gory details, the tragic endings and the moral of the tales. The whole audience was spellbound by a storyteller using material well known to English ears, yet still sounding fresh and amusing as though it were heard by each member of the audience for the first time.

It served as an illustration that the truly great Lieder singers have the ability to communicate a composer's sense of humour, instead of leaving an audience to guess whether they should laugh or not. Fischer-Dieskau could do that and most certainly so can Anne Sofie von Otter.

PHILIP OWEN

As an historian of seventeenth- and eighteenth-century European court culture, I am particularly indebted to Wigmore Hall. It is difficult to imagine the emergence of early-music studies without the active support of Wigmore Hall. It has been the natural home for groups such as Reinhard Goebel's Musica Antiqua Köln and, more recently, the Akademie für Alte Musik from Berlin, not to mention the frequent presence of Monica Huggett and the various manifestations of Sonnerie. It is one thing to read the music, quite another to listen to it. Both activities must go hand-in-hand, and the Wigmore has made an incalculable scholarly contribution in opening our ears to the sounds of the early-modern period.

Moving from the academic to the personal, Wigmore Hall has been a place for making new acquaintances but also for saying farewell to some treasured old friends. During the recent crisis of opera in London it has provided a venue for Christine Schäfer, Angelika Kirchschlager and Juliane Banse, whom the rest of Europe has seen on the stage, while providing

Joshua Bell

Alicia de Larrocha

the opportunity for such a celebrated concert violinist as Joshua Bell to offer his remarkable gifts. The special atmosphere of Wigmore Hall has encouraged combinations of music making amongst friends and colleagues, Bell and Steven Isserlis, but also Jean-Yves Thibaudet, András Schiff, Pascal Rogé. That Alicia de Larrocha, a pianistic augustitude from an earlier generation, should regularly return to Wigmore Hall speaks volumes not simply for its acoustics but also for its special, but intangible and indefinable, atmosphere. These have been exhilarating evenings, emotionally but also intellectually.

Slightly sadder have been the farewells. Of coure, I was fully conscious that the recitals by Sena Jurinac, Régine Crespin (a staggeringly generously performed encore of Frank Bridge's 'Love goes-a-riding') and Ernst Häfliger with his penetrating *Winterreise*, accompanied by his son, Andreas, would be the last time I would see these artists, who had been part of my life and cultural consciousness since the mid-1950s, on any stage. The memories of past decades flooded back, but I would like to finish with two sunnier episodes. The first a rapturously elegiac rendition of a song written by Ned Rorem and performed by the then very young François Le Roux on the potentially commonplace theme of Sunday in Central Park; and what was, incredibly, Anna Tomowa-Sintow's recital debut in London. Following what could have been a master class in Lieder singing, Tomowa-Sintow took over the piano and accompanied herself in a Bulgarian folksong for an encore, with such radiant good humour that the 'ernstlich' and the 'fröhlich' intermingled in a way that has always characterised Wigmore Hall, the genial, loving but also erudite rapport between artists and audiences which the French would call 'une complicité parfaite'.

DR ROBERT ORESKO

Wigmore Hall has long been known as a place where discriminating performers love to sing and play, and where discriminating music lovers choose to come and hear celebrated and often beloved musicians perform. It is equally a place where one might hear an early performance by an artist bound to become celebrated but at this stage of his or her career less widely known.

My biggest love musically and in terms of Wigmore programming is the song recital, and one of my most treasured Wigmore memories my first experience of the gorgeous artistry of Matthias Goerne. At this time, January 1997, he was certainly becoming well-known but had not achieved the place he now surely occupies as the foremost Lieder singer of his (or any current?) generation, and for me this performance of *Winterreise* with Irwin Gage revealed an artist with vocal and particularly interpretative gifts quite extraordinary in one still so young (at this time, I think, about 30).

Maturity is, indeed, the word that seems most immediately appropriate for Goerne's abilities, his performance of Schubert's dark and disturbing masterpiece of emotional pain and psychic disintegration combining absolute vocal beauty and an approach of anguished psychological identification and understanding. There was, indeed, something almost disturbing in his ability to produce such a felt and communicated performance of this work at this stage in his career, a psychological precocity, perhaps. But there was no doubt to my ears that it was an authentic ability, a real understanding, a capacity to express and share that understanding with an audience.

DAVID RICHARDS

This is very much an Anniversary story. We were soon to celebrate our Silver, but had failed to come up with an unusual idea to make it special. Then serendipity stepped in. The Friends newsletter told us that one of our favourite singers would be giving a recital at the Wigmore on 2 March 1999, the eve of the great day.

We invited everyone immediately, then held our breath to see the published programme. Not many of our gang go to Lieder recitals. A few are strangers to concerts. Cross fingers it wouldn't be an advanced, demanding, challenging programme. But serendipity stood by us. There was to be a bit of Poulenc, but otherwise the choice was absolutely ideal. It was the kind of music which is both beginning and end – wonderfully inviting for newcomers, but offering a culminating experience for the initiated.

We had a fabulous evening, with constant high points – meeting everyone in the foyer, champagne in the interval, dining afterwards at Oceana. But the heart of the experience, the emotion that made it unforgettable, was being able to share such singing with our closest friends.

For the artist was Ann Murray. She can hold an audience in so many ways – her blazing concentration, living of the words, sublimely beautiful sound, dramatic truth. Lucky us, to hear her float out Schubert's blissful *Du bist die Ruh*, and enter into the deep sorrowfulness of Mahler's *Ich bin der Welt abhanden gekommen*. I had previously thought Schubert's *Lachen und Weinen* (laughing and crying) rather lightweight, and was shown my mistake.

It's difficult to say whether we were more moved by just sitting and listening, or by the visible impact of the music on our guests. One lovely friend (though a bit of a stubborn Yorkshireman) had previously resisted being introduced to Lieder. He couldn't get out of attending, of course – and then at the interval confessed to being 'gobsmacked' and moved to his depths. I wish I could remember everything people said, but I was much too shaken and stirred.

People say of high excitement, 'it will end in tears'. And so it did. Ann Murray closed the recital with Irish songs, switching us from 'Lachen' with *Ach I dunno*, to 'Weinen' with *She moved thro' the fair*. But those aren't the tears I mean.

My sister had secretly written to her to tell her of our celebration, with the sort of inhibition that my awe at her artistry would forbid. Imagine these two innocent parties, celebrating their big event, sitting in the front row, clapping their hearts out as the encores proceeded, and then hearing her say something along the lines of: 'It is not the usual Wigmore Hall practice to give dedications, but I'm sure William Lyne will forgive me if I dedicate my last encore to two people who are celebrating their Silver Anniversary tonight – Beryl and Ric.' And she sang *Danny Boy*.

BERYL MCALHONE

*W*IGMORE
HALL

SONG RECITAL SERIES

Tuesday 2 March 1999 at 7.30 pm

ANN MURRAY
mezzo soprano

GRAHAM JOHNSON
piano

Supported by the Patron Friends of Wigmore Hall

PROGRAMME
Would patrons please stifle coughing as much as possible
and ensure that watch alarms, mobile phones and any other
electrical devices which can become audible are switched off

	Arie antiche
ANTONIO CALDARA (c.1670-1736)	Selve amiche
ANTONIO LOTTI (c.1667-1740)	Pur dicesti, o bocca bella
CHRISTOPH WILLIBALD VON GLUCK (1714-1787)	O del mio dolce ardor from *Paride ed Elena*
GEORGE FRIDERIC HANDEL (1685-1759)	Ombra mai fù from *Xerxes*
JOHANNES SIMON MAYR (1763-1845)	Variations on Paisiello's 'Nel cor più non mi sento'
	Settings of poems by Friedrich Rückert
FRANZ SCHUBERT (1797-1828)	Lachen und Weinen • Du bist die Ruh'
ROBERT SCHUMANN (1810-1856)	Widmung • O ihr Herren • Volksliedchen
GUSTAV MAHLER (1860-1911)	Ich atmet' einen linden Duft • Blicke mir nicht in die Lieder!
	Ich bin der Welt abhanden gekommen
	INTERVAL
FRANCIS POULENC (1899-1963)	La grenouillère
	Tu vois le feu du soir
	La fraîcheur et le feu
	Quatre poèmes de Guillaume Apollinaire
	L'anguille • Carte postale • Avant le cinéma • 1904
IRISH FOLK SONGS	The Spanish Lady
	The Last Rose of Summer (arr. Stevenson)
	Ach, I dunno
	She moved thro' the Fair
	Phil the Fluter's Ball

Wigmore Hall Director: William Lyne MBE, Hon. FTCL, Hon. GSM
Lessees: City of Westminster • The Wigmore Hall Trust
Registered Charity No.1024838
Cover design by Peter Williamson
PROGRAMME: £2.00

Ann Murray's programme for 2 March 1999

Andrew Payne

More than just a Music Hall

Not content with being one of the world's leading chamber music and recital halls of the last hundred years, Wigmore Hall (née Bechstein, of course) has also endeavoured to entice a wider audience through its staging of 'extra-curricular' events, more commonly seen elsewhere. Often surprising (and sometimes arguably unwise), such diversions from the classical norm present a fascinating insight into the shifting mindset of twentieth-century society, in a way the specialist music events perhaps cannot. And while music has always been the guiding spirit of the Hall, the music heard within its hallowed walls has not always been by Schubert and Britten etc., and it has certainly not always been beautiful. For Noël Coward has also had his say; the accordion, hurdy-gurdy and hand-bell have all brought forth their questionable tones, to let the Hall's famed acoustics do what they can; and there was once an evening of Alpine yodelling.

When the Bechstein Hall opened its doors in 1901 it did so primarily to the upper classes. Steps towards equality in society, which were to be accelerated by the horrors of World War I, were as yet in their infancy. Great Britain was still the most powerful nation on earth, with the largest empire the world had seen, and London's well-to-do, its 'idle rich', seemed to be in control of it all. That is presumably why most of the events at the Hall in the 1900s began at 3 pm, when *only* the unemployed (and we are not talking about out-of-work dockers) would be able to attend. The old queen was dead, but Victorian high society still enjoyed its musical soirées and 'at homes' as it had always done, and it was evidently still able to afford Bechstein's pianos. However, even the aristocracy needed its light relief, and that usually meant Music Hall.

Music Hall: with its top hats and turns, gavels and groans, thunderous voices and petticoat innocence, gymnasts and bombasts, ventriloquists and humorists. Immensely popular with all sections of society, a slightly

BECHSTEIN HALL,
WIGMORE STREET, LONDON, W.

Programme of
Mr.
Harrison Hill's
Humorous and Musical
Recital
(Under the direction of the Lecture Agency, Ltd.).

MONDAY, OCT. 28th, 1901,
AT 8.30 O'CLOCK.

Humorous recital by Mr Harrison Hill

more sophisticated(?) form of Music Hall entertainment hit the Bechstein Hall stage for the first time on 28 October 1901, with A Humorous Recital by Harrison Hill. Items included a topical song 'on subjects in today's papers', an impersonation of Joseph Chamberlain entitled 'My Distinguished Double' (the impression amounted to Harrison Hill inserting a monocle in one eye) and 'My Juliet – A Shakespearean Coon Song'. Mr Hill also performed his own patriotic song, 'True to England', which began: 'All who are proud of England, / Come sing a song with me, / Here's to the land that gave us birth, / Land of the brave and free.' The evening presumably proved popular, for Harrison Hill was soon to return, though this time as one act of many, in Charles Capper's Musical & Dramatic Entertainment in March 1902. Pure Music Hall, the proceedings began at 8.30 pm with Mr Capper's famed whistling solos (the programme advertised the artiste's own book *The Art of Whistling*). His brother Alfred followed with a Thought Reading Seance, after which came 29 other items including imitations, short stories, masked singers and a Glassophone Solo. Carriages at 11.45 pm!

Harrison Hill and the Cappers dominated this kind of entertainment throughout the 1900s, but they were not entirely without rivals. There was Miss Beatrice Stuart's Concert Party, for instance, which gave a Farewell Concert prior to their tour in South Africa – sea travel meant the entertainers might not return for years. There were the Misses Atkinson and Bowick, whose repertoire in December 1901 included 'Marguerite (A chat with a French waitress)', and Mr Ulph Smith, of whom the *Daily Telegraph* said in 1903: 'Mr Smith revealed an exceedingly happy knack for converting a secular melody turn by turn into a church voluntary, a

hymn, a dirge, and a wedding march, to the manifest delight of his listeners.' Ulph Smith's most successful musical sketch was 'Oh! That
Miller's Daughter', which was first performed shortly after Schubert's *Die
schöne Müllerin* had first been heard at the Hall. Unfortunately the words
are not printed so there is no way of telling whether Smith's was a parody of Schubert's. At the end of every event 'God Save the King' was sung,
sometimes, as after the Moray Minstrels had given a Ladies' Night variety show, with a second verse printed in the programme.

By 1909, performing in costume had become a prominently advertised
element of such entertainments. The Austin Dobson Costume Recital of
Music Hall sketches in November of that year was soon followed by
Béatrice von Holthoir's matinée performance of her latest speciality,
18th century Bergerettes in French costume. The Bergerettes were described as 'drawing room playlets . . . dainty, amusing trifles.'

With costume, of course, came dancing, and although the size of the
stage should have precluded any of it, there have been a few brave enough
to risk its confines. An astonishing event was the appearance of the Dream-
dancer, Madeleine Grasnojada, in 1910. A 'Sensational Scientific Pheno-
menon', she executed 'in a state of sleep the most perfect dances.' Asleep?
Brave indeed! More conventionally, two Russian ballet dancers, Nadine
Nicolayeva and Nicholas Legat, performed in aid of Serbian Relief in
December 1914, and a year later Miss Winnie Lack gave a variety of dances
in aid of the British Red Cross. In 1918, Serafina Astafieva brought her
entire dancing school with her.

It was not only during wartime that promoters felt impelled to label
their events in aid of some charity or other. As early as 1901 there was a
concert for the Institute of Massage by the Blind, whose programme
stressed the advantages of receiving a massage from a blind person, who
would have a heightened sense of touch, thus being particularly sensitive
to the knots in one's back. Massage, it concluded, was the most appropriate means of employment for what was a largely unemployed section
of society. Other worthy causes included in 1904 the Emily Harris Home,
which 'offers safe lodging to young working girls . . . obliged to live away
from their homes'; the Poor of the Parish of St George-in-the-East in
1909; and the National Anti-Vivisection Hospital in 1910. During World
War I, however, it was a rare event that was not given with charity in

mind. Beneficiaries included the Belgian Relief Fund, St. Dunstan's Blinded Soldiers & Sailors Hostel in Regent's Park, the Royal Waterloo Hospital 'which the War has sadly crippled financially', Prisoners of War of the Middlesex Regiment, the Russian Prisoners' Bread Fund, and the Church Army's Recreation Huts & Tents, whose aim was 'to furnish food, drink, comfort and rest – a priceless boon, especially to the walking wounded.'

World War I prompted vehement anti-German feelings in Britain, which eventually led to the Bechstein Hall's closure in 1915. Wartime concerts advertised 'All-Allied' programmes and when Archy Rosenthal gave a recital in the re-opened Wigmore Hall in 1917 the programme stated quite clearly that, despite his surname, the pianist was 'British both by Birth & Parentage'. The dreadfulness of the times is obvious even from the concert programmes, but there was still room for light-heartedness, especially when the Pierrots of the 25th Division, who often acted as stretcher-bearers at the front, gave a series of entertainments at the Hall during the last two years of the war. Formed to keep the troops happy, items in the programmes included 'When the Boys go marching back to Blighty', 'Ting-a-Ling', and 'Beautiful Girlie Girls'.

With the return of peace in 1918 most people no doubt wished to be distracted from the horrors of recent experience, while at the same time the scars of war must have been apparent on every thoroughfare, including Wigmore Street. There were also demands from the lower classes for some sort of reward for the enormous sacrifices they had made. A combination of all these things gave rise to a remarkable series of concerts given in aid of the Adair Wounded Fund. Entitled Sunday Socials, a glittering array of diverse entertainments was witnessed by a much lower class audience. There were humorists, whistlers, ventriloquists, conjurors, versatile comediennes, mimics, concertina players, accordionists, song mummers, wine glass performers, Alpine yodellers and many others. Members of the audience were 'earnestly requested not to leave their seats or walk down the gangways whilst a turn is in progress.' During each evening a Lucky Draw took place. Prizewinners could look forward to such delights as a case of oranges, Virginia cigs, a silk handkerchief, a box of figs, a basket of chestnuts, socks, second-hand clothes, a ball of string, a Briar pipe, a week's holiday at Margate, a pair of military hair-

"A good laugh is worth a donkey-load of medicine."
— ANON.

ROB WILKIN'S JAZZ BAND
THE SEVEN CRACKER-JACKS
(Including the Old Gentleman Himself)
will give Selections at Intervals.

Artistes:

Evelyn Clifford	Contralto ⎱ In Duets
John Humphreys	Baritone ⎰
The Brompton Quartette	Male Voice Quartette
Hetty Bolton	Pianist
Dinkie Jeune	Light Comedy Vocalist
James Chilcott	Humorist
Kathleen Musker	Siffleuse
Cliff Lester	Whimsical Wizard
R. Woodhouse Pitman	Conjuror
"Gerrard"	Diabolist

and

Wilson James' Company	Marcia Bourn	Soprano
	George Stockwin	Baritone
"THE GAIETIES"	Eileen Dare	Soubrette
	Mabel Adeane	Comedienne
under the direction of	Dennis Martin	Humorist
Frederic Groome	Frederic Groome	Entertainer
	Sydney Jerome	Pianist

Accompanists:

Richard Tonking   Sydney Warwick

Musical Directors   -   Frederic Groome & Alec Bell

Smoking now disallowed in the Hall, owing to the damage done to the Carpets.

Cigarettes will be distributed as usual, but not until after the Concert.

"A little nonsense now and then is relished by the best of men."
— BYRON.

LUCKY DRAW.

HOSPITALS.

Winning Numbers.
1. A Self-filling Fountain Pen, a jar of Salmon & Anchovy Paste, and a pair of Braces.
2. A Thermos Flask with 2 Cups, a box of Chocolate Biscuits and 1 Lead and 1 Indelible Pencil.
3. A Game of Rope Quoits, a jar of Honey and 3 Bandana Handkerchiefs.
4. A Pocket Scissors, Knife and File in Case, a tin of Sardines and a packet of Stamped Envelopes.
5. An Electric Torch, a pot of Plum Jam and a bottle of Brilliantine.
6. A Shaving Bowl, a packet of Stamped Post-cards and a Silk Knitted Tie.
7. A Tin of Fancy Biscuits, a 2/- Postal Order and a packet of Studs.

DRIVERS.

1. A bottle of Old Douro Port and a La Corona Cigar.
2. A bottle of Old Douro Port and a few Cigarettes.

CONSOLATION PRIZES.

The Gifts presented by
Miss Rosalie Carr-Jackson and Friends.

TEA (this week)

Manor House Orthopaedic Hospital, Hampstead	Lyons'
Ducane Road Hospital, Shepherd's Bush	Maison Riche,
The Queen's Hospital, Sidcup	Regent Street,
Roehampton House, Roehampton	W.
Church Lane Hospital, Tooting	Lyons'
Disabled Soldiers Embroidery Industry, Ebury Street, S.W.	474, Oxford Street, W.
Royal Herbert Hospital, Woolwich	Pritchards,
South African Hospital, Richmond Park	79, Oxford Street, W

Adair Wounded Fund programme

brushes in a case and an IOU for 6s & 8d. Our amusement at the start of the 21st century should perhaps be tempered by the fact that the Adair Wounded Fund, which was registered under the War Charities Act to give regular entertainment to hospital invalids still undergoing treatment for wounds received in the Great War, gave its 404th, and last, Sunday Social at Wigmore Hall as late as 1938, only a year before the next, even greater, war was to begin. By the late 1930s whistlers sadly no longer appeared, but the prizes were as imaginative as ever: a pair of bootlaces, something for the wife, a haddock, a box of smokes and Black Magic chocs. A box of smokes may have been a prize in 1938 but the lucky winner would not have been allowed to smoke the contents during the entertainment, for, as long ago as 1922, after two years of warning careless smokers, a Sunday Social programme stated that 'Smoking is now disallowed in the Hall, owing to the damage done to the upholstery & carpets. Cigarettes will be distributed but not until after the concert.'

One assumes that cigarettes were sold and not given away, thereby

joining a long list of merchandise and services which have been promoted through the Hall. In 1902 Mrs Montague Fordham stated on the
leaflet advertising her vocal recital that she 'desires to obtain engage-
ments for At Homes'. Tickets for the recital itself were available directly
from Mrs Fordham's home address, a common arrangement in those
days. A year later, Mrs Josef Conn's Health Exercises were promoted by
way of a demonstration-recital. The programme is comic in the extreme,
with its before-and-after shots of a young girl slumping her shoulders
and frowning and then *not* slumping her shoulders and smiling, in order
to show the *amazing* improvements brought about by the exercises:
'[*Before*] The above figure illustrates the position so often assumed by
growing girls . . . which in time must lead to serious results. [*After*] This
is the same figure evenly developed, with erect head, prominent chest &
symmetrical, corsetless waist.' The miraculous effects must have been
instantaneous as the girl does not look a day older in the second photograph and is still wearing the same blouse. Other promotions included
the many pupils' concerts (the last one was in 1971), always organised by
the teacher, in order to sell their skills to parents ever hopeful of their off-

Mrs Conn's Exercises: Before and After

springs' talents, and record recitals, which sold records of course, but also gramophones, from their invention right up to the 1980s. In 1903 the Triumph Piano-Player had the stage to itself for an evening, claiming to be 'the most marvellous invention of this age of progress . . . The Triumph supplies the technique, and that in a faultless manner; while the nuances etc., which contribute to what is known as an expressive rendering will be coloured with the individuality of the human being who is playing it.' Competition came from the Angelus in 1904. In 1922 the London School of Dalcroze Eurythmics sold its services with a lecture-demonstration: 'Before teaching music to a child the teacher should endeavour to awaken his whole organism . . . co-ordinate his nervous motor impulses according to the laws of Measure . . . and develop his sensitiveness to shades of force.' My own favourite sales pitch, however, appeared on the Hall's monthly diaries in 1985, advertising car stickers with such catchy slogans as 'Wigmore Hall . . . Sounds Marvellous' and 'Wigmore Coffee Concerts . . . the cream in music'. A bargain at 20p each.

Demonstrations and lectures have been commonplace throughout the Hall's history; events of this type were not always as focused as they are today, though no less interesting. Some have had a musical slant, such as in 1909 Herman Klein's Candid & Impartial Lecture: The Truth about Music in America; a lecture in 1917 on the Principles Underlying Dr Yorke Trotter's Rhythmic Method; or Maria Callas: Personal reminiscences by Robert Sutherland, in 1980. Others have not, including Samuel Aitken's lecture in 1901, The Story of the First Ascent of Mount St Elias, with photographic lantern slides; three lectures on the war given by John Buchan in 1915, with the Rt. Hon. Arthur Balfour MP presiding; another war lecture, in French, in 1917, with discussion by Hilaire Belloc; and a lecture given by the Congress of the Chartered Soc. of Massage & Medical Gymnastics entitled 'Internal Secretions'! Other organisations have held important meetings at the Hall over the years, including The Women's Reserve Ambulance (the very last event at the Hall before closure in 1915), the Southern Railway Corporation in the 1950s, and Trinity College of Music, which has held prizegiving events here for many years.

Politics has remained largely outside the Hall's extensive repertoire, but one organisation to give it prominence was the Friends of Italy. Formed in the early 1920s by Captain Charles Foxcroft MP, a man of

'Friends of Italy' at Home

missionary zeal, the events promised 'A Delightful Musical Afternoon'. What is of interest here is the overtly political nature of the editorials printed in the programmes, while the organisation claimed to be *non-political*. Bullish quotations from Benito Mussolini about the wonders of Fascism appeared alongside useful comments by Captain Foxcroft: 'One feature of the *fascista* regime worth mentioning, as showing what discipline can do, is the practical disappearance of strikes and the reduction of 75% of pilferage.' Running for many years, the Friends of Italy finally succumbed to the turning tide in 1938. Its last programme proudly stated that: 'Today Italy, renovated in spirit and faith, guided on the path to the highest conquest by the genius of an incomparable leader . . . it will ever be a source of pride for Italy to advance by the side of powerful Britain towards the highest summit of human civilisation.' The very next year Italy and Britain locked horns against each other and were at war.

During World War II events of any kind were greatly reduced in number. Those that took place again reflected both the charitable and xenophobic nature of Britain in wartime. Pianist Franz Wagner was pointedly described as Czechoslovakian and there were concerts in aid of the Free Austrian Movement and various groups of refugees. Remarkably, in the midst of war in 1943, a recital was held in aid of the People's Dispensary for Sick Animals, which says much about the English. Only one extra-curricular event stands out during World War II, a Grand Concert under the auspices of the London Cab & Omnibus (Horse) Drivers' Aid Association, featuring Dorothy & Helen, The Monday Night at Eight Girls, and comedian Charles Coburn, 'Old-time Music Hall favourite of *The Man who broke the bank at Monte Carlo* fame.'

The aftermath of war was characterised for many by deprivation, rationing and dashed hopes. Those who could not face the music often turned to religion, also catered for at Wigmore Hall. Spiritual matters had been aired here before. In 1917 there was both a Liberal Jewish Synagogue Service and a Theosophical Society Lecture on Death and the Resurrection. In 1937 the Montreal-based Temple of Service brought 'all walks of life and all manners of thought and religion' together at the Hall to promote common understanding and world peace. Its motto was 'Do not accept anything until you realise it to be the truth.' There was a membership application form in the programme, the only obligation being 'to serve my fellow men to the best of my ability', and some money. Where the Temple of Service patently failed, after the war Dr Emmet Fox aimed to do better, forming his New Thought Alliance and sharing his philosophy with a Wigmore audience in 1947. The Jewish community responded by holding Jewish High Holy Day Services here in the same year, and every Sunday evening for the next decade a Spiritualistic Service took place, complete with seances, thought-readings and doubtless a miracle or two. A forerunner of this kind of 'entertainment' had occurred in 1938, when Josef Marion displayed his 'genuine gifts . . . tested by the University of London Council for Psychical Investigation' by informing members of the audience who they were and facts about their life from nothing more than a hair off their head or a sample of their handwriting.

If spiritual relief was not forthcoming perhaps the 'viewless wings of poesy' might improve matters. Certainly a concerted effort was made when, on 14 May 1947, one of the most remarkable line-ups ever seen on the Wigmore stage appeared for a poetry recital. Poets including Dylan Thomas, Cecil Day Lewis, Louis MacNeice, Walter de la Mare, T. S. Eliot, Edith Sitwell and poet laureate John Masefield all read their own works, and actors no less luminary than Edith Evans and John Gielgud made tangible those of other great writers. Twenty years later John Gielgud returned, this time alongside Peggy Ashcroft, for another poetic entertainment entitled 'Cardinal Virtues, Deadly Sins'. In 1976 the Hall host-ed a whole week of chamber music and poetry. While poetry has not been recited much since then, at least it has been sung frequently.

Actors of varying abilities appeared throughout the Hall's early histo-ry. Mrs Tobias Matthay gave a dramatic recital of serious scenes in 1903, Laura Stubbing's (elocutionist) recitations in 1909 included Longfellow's *Death of Minnehaha*, and in 1910, Max Montor (actor-manager of the Schauspielhaus in Hamburg) recited modern works in German and in costume. 1917 saw a three-night run of an Early English Nativity Play with Ellen Terry, complete with a procession of saints and martyrs, and performances of the Miracle Plays of Medieval York. Plays by the great Indian writer Rabindranath Tagore were staged by an all-British cast in 1921. More recently, the likes of Prunella Scales ('An Evening with Queen Victoria'), Terry Jones (of *Monty Python* fame) and Eleanor Bron have graced the stage.

Recent decades have seen the Hall sticking firmly to the curriculum. Almost. Folk singers had their heyday in the 60s and 70s; jazz has come and gone and thankfully come back again; and Ravi Shankar and Larry Adler have long since exited stage left. Odd events such as 'Pitch' in 1971, described as music and poetry as sound and action, with items including 'The Story of an Apple Pie', 'Boating Song' and 'Bloating Song', have come along occasionally to keep at least this researcher on his toes, and Bob Downes did his best in the 70s with evenings of music, mime, drama, lateral thinking and symbolism! If there has been an extra-curricular development in recent times it is the growth of comedy, recently des-cribed as the bindweed of the Edinburgh Fringe. Here, laughter has been induced by David Kossoff in 1976, Hinge & Bracket, the Parlour Quartet (costume Victoriana) and the Cambridge Buskers in the 70s and 80s, and Barry Humphries, with sidekicks Dame Edna Everage and Sir Les Pat-terson, in 1997. Most recently it was Kit & the Widow, who will forgive me if I say that something about the Widow in particular reminds me of Queen Victoria and takes me right back to 1901.

The above forms just a selection of the out-of-the-ordinary events which have taken place at Wigmore Hall. If there is too great an empha-sis on the first half of the twentieth century that is because those years provide not only a wider variety from which to choose but also events of greater interest, at least to my mind, due to the distance of time and mindset. At various times a playhouse, a fancy-dress, a dance studio, a collection box, a variety show, a lottery, a shop, a lecture theatre, a mouth-piece, a temple, a comedy store, and always a stage, Wigmore Hall has witnessed and played a part in the life of a very broad community indeed. As a centre for such diverse art forms (the term should be used guarded-ly with some of the examples here given) it is, and always has been, a great deal more than just a music hall.

Behind the Scenes at Wigmore Hall

*All the photographs used in this section were taken by Jim Four
at Wigmore Education Department and Cavatina Chamber Music Trust events*

The Box Office

'Good afternoon, Wigmore Hall, can I help you?' Words that are familiar to many readers of this book, but what *does* go on behind the scenes in the Box Office?

I like to think of the Box Office as one of the most important departments in the whole operation that is Wigmore Hall, as we are the first point of contact that people have with the organisation, and if they are not looked after satisfactorily it will affect their whole attitude to the venue. When interviewing any new staff members we recognise the importance of a good knowledge of classical music, as it is vital at least to be able to pronounce correctly the names of composers, even if the names of some artists pose a few problems! Most of the staff have musical backgrounds, and are either trying to make ends meet until they manage to get professional jobs (such as in the Glyndebourne chorus) or have decided to pursue a career in arts management rather than one in performance.

One of the unique features of Wigmore Hall is the regularity of so many of the audience; even after eleven years in the Box Office I still find myself saying 'Oh, so *you* are so-and-so' when a patron with a familiar name comes to the window. You do, of course, get to remember where some people like to sit (mostly the front few rows crowd!), but then you get people saying 'My normal seats please,' which with a data base of almost 80,000 records is not always much help to us!

A high proportion of bookings dealt with by the Box Office takes place during priority booking periods. On occasions, demand for certain concerts will outstrip ticket availability, often several times over, which we are well aware leads to much disappointment. It is hard to send an envelope to someone with no tickets inside when all the concerts they applied for have sold out, as was sometimes the case during the Centenary Festival booking period. You then get the telephone calls: 'I asked for a certain seat and have not been given it for three of the concerts,' or 'You must have made a mistake' (in hurt tones). Of course we always take complaints seriously and it is those calls which stick in the mind, but it is so refreshing when somebody makes the effort to call and say, 'Thank you, I got everything I wanted.' And we do get encouraging feedback from patrons,

Schools concert

giving us comments along the lines of 'the most helpful Box Office around' or 'Your staff are always charming and patient.' Some people choose to show their gratitude at Christmas time which is always appreciated!

I do smile inwardly when a patron comes up to the window on the evening of a concert saying, 'I have done the most awful thing and left the tickets at home. What can you do?', then see the look of astonishment when a few seconds later duplicate tickets come out of the printer. It is certainly one of the advantages of having a computerised ticketing system. People sometimes ask 'Why do you need my name?' and this is one very good reason why. It also makes it possible for us to try and contact everyone if a concert is cancelled. On the occasion of a sold-out concert there is often quite a demand for returned tickets, which we will always try to sell for people if a concert is fully booked. You stand the best chance of having tickets resold if you send them back in plenty of time, but we do understand that this may not always be possible, as often illness or emergencies are not known about until the last minute.

With the introduction during 2000 of the Wigmore Hall website (*www.wigmore-hall.org.uk*) we are always looking for new ways to give patrons better service. At the time of writing, bookings can be made by fax through the internet, and perhaps in the near future we may be able to have secure e-mail booking online as well.

In so many ways the Box Office is the main link with the audience. You need us to get into the concerts and we need you in order to have something to do! May we have many more years of working together as appropriate to our beloved Wigmore Hall.

PETER BLACK, *Box Office Manager*

The House Manager

Wigmore Hall seems to me like a safe home in London. I remember as a student at the Royal College of Music coming for the first time to hear a concert by Shura Cherkassky. I turned up, got a return ticket, and found the whole experience quite magical – what better introduction to Wigmore Hall than the ever-unpredictable and exciting Cherkassky! And then on 27 December 1985 I joined the staff as one of the Concert Assistants, which involved working in the Box Office during the day and acting as duty House Manager in the evening on a rota basis. The entire staff then consisted of Director, Assistant Director, secretary, three Concert Assistants, two part-time Box Office assistants, three cleaners and a caretaker. What a change from today!

I was trained for my house management duties by William Lyne, and remember well my first evening 'going solo', a concert by the Beaux Arts Trio. The page-turner did not appear, so I had to stand-in and do that job as well. Menahem Pressler was wonderful; I was far more nervous than he was and he calmed me down and looked after me – it should really have been the other way around! It was a baptism of fire for one of the prime requirements of the House Manager, which is the ability to think on your feet and adapt to whatever situation arises.

It is the House Manager's responsibility to see that everything is 'all right on the night' and that the evening runs smoothly. Crises, both large and small, tend to happen in the last hour before the concert, which usually means sorting out foyer problems, answering queries, supervising the ushers, and, most importantly, seeing to the needs of the artists. It is obviously essential for the House Manager to be as relaxed as possible, whatever the circumstances, and to create a supportive environment for the artists of the evening. The familiar walk up the right aisle a few minutes before the start of the concert is the moment when the House Manager makes a final check to see that all is well with the performers, that the lighting is adjusted for the platform and the Hall, and that everything is ready for the concert to begin, a procedure which now includes a reminder to the audience to switch off all mobile phones!

The building of warm relationships with the artists is vital; continuity is appreciated and when the House Manager is a familiar face there is a sense of security and that 'family feeling' which is one of the Hall's great strengths. So many of the artists speak of 'coming home' when they return. The fact, too, that the House Manager knows many of the audience by name and not just by sight adds to this feeling of intimacy. The House Manager of the evening (there are three of us altogether) often has the support of Giorgio Liu, the ever-cheerful and invaluable Commissionaire-cum-caretaker, whose many skills are frequently called on in moments of crisis. John Allchurch is another familiar figure at the door, who has been greeting the audience now for thirteen years.

Concerts may hold many surprises. I remember Leslie Howard's astonishment at his 50th birthday concert when I came on stage bearing a cake and then sat at the piano to play 'Happy Birthday' for the whole audience to join in singing. There was a cake, too, for Cherkassky at his 75th birthday concert – this time in the shape of a grand piano! No one evening is ever the same as another, nothing can be totally planned down to the very last detail, however hard you try. But that is one of the pleasures of the job. The evening ends for the House Manager when the concert is over, the artists and audience have left, the building is checked throughout, computers are switched off, the doors are locked, and another successful concert has played its part in the Wigmore's 100-year history.

DAVID KING, *Senior House Manager*

The Wigmore Hall Flowers

My association with the Wigmore Hall now spans some 17 years. My first appearance there (as a florist) was while working for a company that then supplied all the flowers for stage, foyer and presentation. So for two years I attended to the flowers at the Hall on a weekly basis before taking on the contract myself 15 years ago.

In those early days the Wigmore Hall was then supported by the Arts Council of Great Britain. William Lyne was not yet honoured with an MBE, Vi Gray was bringing her own inimitable style to the ladies' loo – excuse me, the 'Powder Room' – and I was able to leap in one swift bound from auditorium floor to stage and back again in the bat of an eyelid!

The Front of House team, along with George Ross who was then Caretaker, did much to make me feel welcome in the early days when I took over the contract. Paul Davies, who later went on to be General Manager at St John's, Smith Square, was particularly helpful in assisting me with my endeavours to learn about the workings of the Hall. He

Holiday workshop

possessed a wicked sense of humour and for some time I was blissfully unaware that everyone associated with the Hall was given a nickname. It was some while before I discovered that mine was 'Carmen'! Whether this was because at that time I smoked or because of my temperament, which could be fiery, I dread to think. One thing for sure, however, it was nothing to do with my latent talent with the castanets!

Right from the beginning I was quite sure in my own mind that the flowers for the Hall should be an integral part of the overall setting and not stand apart from it. For that reason, the style of the stage flowers has remained unchanged for all these years, reflecting instead the classic surroundings of a Victorian concert hall. Our main agenda has always been good quality, good value, and to provide arrangements that neither hinder nor detract from the performers. We try always to look for flowers which shed little pollen and are unscented, both of which can be a difficulty for performers, especially the singers. In some ways we are limited in our choice of flowers and also have to bear in mind that they must last a full week – not easy when every night they are under the spotlights. From what we hear, however, over the years we seem to have got it right for most of the time, although not always.

At Christmas time we tend to let our hair down with the decorations for the Hall, and sparkle and glitz have become our trademark of the festive season, usually to much joy and critical acclaim – although not from everyone. One prima donna refused to go on stage unless my arrangements came off! She felt they were far too 'over the top' for a Christmas concert. Panic ensued backstage and there was no choice for those concerned but to remove them from either side of the stage to the Green Room. This act of indulgence towards an artist only highlights the care, concern and attention performers receive from all the staff at the Wigmore Hall and it is a reputation that they have long held.

And so had *this* diva been upset? To the contrary. I experienced a perverse sense of joy at the thought of nearly stopping the show! And the next day my arrangements were returned to their rightful place on stage and remained there for the rest of the Christmas period. This had been the one and only time there were no flowers on stage for a performance.

We supply all the house bouquets for presentation on stage and very often they will consist of all one type of flower, for example a profusion of roses. It is always our practice as florists to remove all thorns from roses for presentation for obvious reasons. However, at one recital, at which I was present, I watched eagerly as a beautiful bouquet of roses we had prepared was presented to a Dutch soprano who was so popular at the Hall. As she received the bouquet and clasped it to her bosom, her expression briefly but obviously changed from one of gratitude to one of pain. I knew what had happened. A thorn had escaped the system and pierced her. I sat mortified in the audience as I watched for signs of blood. After the performance I was taken backstage by the House Manager to meet her. To my embarrassment I was introduced as the House Florist as he enquired whether she was pleased with her bouquet. Smiling sweetly she thanked him for the most beautiful bouquet of roses and, moving to greet another admirer, she then turned directly to me saying, 'I shall never forget the experience of receiving them!'

Many changes have taken place during my years at the Wigmore Hall. Familiar faces have moved on, to be replaced with new ones which, with time, have become familiar. Computerisation has replaced manual ticket delivery, the Wigmore Hall has become a self-funding, charitable organisation and, as my own business has blossomed with time, I have been happy in recent years to lend my own support to the annual fund-raising Charity Gala Evening by donating, if not in full, in part, most of the flowers for that occasion – my show of thanks for a long friendship and working relationship with the Hall.

I have also been privileged over the years to have been given many house tickets for performances of artists that I would otherwise have missed, some of these making their debuts and some their farewell performances. Others, in the case of my dear friends mezzo-soprano Sue Kessler and accompanist Geoffrey Parsons, have gone for good to make great music in a finer place. All have been unmissable.

As for me, music and flowers at the Hall have become an integral part of my life and I look forward to my own continued performance at the Hall for as long as they will have me. My only deference to time is that I now no longer leap from auditorium floor to stage but enter and exit via the stairs!

MALCOLM HAZELL

Music and Time family day

Looking after the Pianos

Piano music is fundamental at Wigmore Hall and it is often said that the Hall's resident orchestra consists of its two Steinway concert grand pianos. These two instruments are in constant use; on stage virtually every day, they are used for rehearsals in the morning and afternoon and then played in evening performances.

With its busy concert season, it is vital that Wigmore Hall has the *right* pianos. The Hall requires instruments that meet not only the demands of the Hall's unique acoustics, but also the demands of the artists who play them. During the season, the pianos are used for a vast repertoire in solo recitals, as accompanying instruments, and as an integral part of chamber music ensembles. The incredible diversity of music demands instruments that are both perfectly maintained and capable of the widest possible breadth of expression.

There are two Steinway model 'D' concert grand pianos resident in Wigmore Hall. The older of the two, 870 (concert and artist pianos are usually referred to by the last 3 digits of their serial numbers), was built in Steinway's Hamburg factory in 1982 and was selected for Wigmore Hall by the late Geoffrey Parsons and Sir Clifford Curzon. Age has given this piano a rich, gentle, and mellow tone and makes it eminently suitable for use as an accompanying instrument and for early repertoire solo work. The younger instrument, 508, was built in Hamburg in 1996, prepared in London along with other potential instruments, and finally selected for Wigmore Hall by András Schiff. This piano offers a fresher sound with tremendous clarity of tone without being either too brilliant or percussive (qualities which, while welcome for the concerto repertoire in large venues, would overwhelm the intimacy of Wigmore Hall) and suits more contemporary repertoire and solo work.

The condition of the pianos is constantly monitored with both action and tone being regularly adjusted and maintained. They are tuned immediately prior to *every* performance (which can mean being tuned three or more times in a day). Major servicing work is co-ordinated by Wigmore Hall's Senior House Manager and the Concert and Artist Department at Steinway Hall. This work is normally carried out at Steinway Hall's basement workshop during the July/August break. Such work has included the fitting of a completely new action in 870 (also known as the 'Old Lady'), ensuring that this older instrument – which has had a lot of wear with its years of daily use – performs with the precision and sensitivity of a new piano and fulfils the highest expectations of the artist. Also, 870's keyboard has been re-covered with 'old stock' ivory as the original keys had worn too thin from constant use. The strings in the top two treble sections have been replaced several times. This prevents the short, thin, high-tension strings from becoming too brittle which results in a thin, metallic tone and the potential to break during a performance. While it is necessary to replace the treble strings every 3 years, part of the 'magic' of the expert technician is in knowing what to leave alone; the tenor and bass strings are all original as they are essential to the mature, mellow tone of this fine old instrument. The 'baby' (508) is still relatively untouched as it continues to enjoy the vigour of youth. However, one special feature is that its artificial keytops have been replaced with 'old stock' ivory giving the keyboard a 'friendlier', more traditional touch.

The challenge is to provide Wigmore Hall with pianos that have distinct characters, but will work either as solo or as accompanying instruments. Wigmore Hall's intimate environment and acoustics – features which inform and shape a performance as much as the artist and his or her instrument – require pianos with a warm, singing tone, full of colour and depth. Only such instruments can sound beautiful and be a credit to both the artist and the exceptional nature of one of the world's premier concert venues.

ULRICH GERHARTZ, *Steinway & Sons*

The Development Department

Patronage of the arts has existed for many centuries and Wigmore Hall continues to build on this tradition. The Hall first employed a fund-raiser in 1991 and since then this vital area of activity has flourished. Almost half of the Hall's total income is raised from corporate and private donors as well as from grant-giving organisations. There is now a dedicated team comprising a Head of Development, a Trusts and Foundations Manager, a Friends Administrator and a Development Co-ordinator. The job of the Development Department is to raise as much money as possible in as many different ways as possible to support the work of the Hall.

Wigmore Hall is unusual amongst its competitors in that public funding forms a very small part of its annual income. Whilst this puts pressure on the fund-raising staff, it also means that the Hall does not have to fulfil numerous criteria to safeguard its public funding in the way that many other arts organisations have to. It is perhaps because of this that the Hall has been able to create its own unique and very powerful identity.

The lack of public funding means that Wigmore Hall increasingly relies on private support to fund the high level of musical activity which it promotes. Without donations from enlightened companies, individuals and trusts, the Hall would have been unable to establish its reputation as one of the finest concert halls in world. The continually increasing Development income reflects a remarkable amount of commitment on the part of donors.

Over the last 100 years, hundreds of supporters have backed Wigmore Hall's mission. One of the most enjoyable things about fund-raising is including donors in the Hall's work in a personal way and making them feel they belong here. Finding out what supporters are really interested in supporting is a crucial part of the department's work. A recent donor said he would support an oboe concert by a young musician which included works by Britten and it is a tribute to the Hall's imaginative and diverse programming that we were able to identify a concert that met all three criteria! It is this sense of involvement which is the key to increasing private income for the Hall.

Supporters of the Hall's work can also benefit from a public profile amongst our audience and access to tickets and entertaining facilities. The Development team does its best to meet all requests – however out

Schools project

of the ordinary. More unusual corporate involvement has included a gospel coaching master class for a company's clients at the Hall.

The Hall's attitude towards its supporters is encapsulated by Dr Donald McLeod, a director of the Change Partnership, one of the Hall's corporate members: 'For us, the relationship has felt right from the start. It is partly a question of scale and partly one of style. In scale, our own business is chamber orchestra sized rather than symphony. And our thrust is all about helping to develop talent. The congruencies are almost too obvious to mention.'

The Development Department looks forward to forming many new relationships with supporters and nurturing existing ones during the forthcoming century.

EMILY STUBBS

The Rubinstein Circle

The Rubinstein Circle was founded four years ago with the aim of helping to provide continuous annual income for the Wigmore Hall.

The idea was to create a group of members who would donate £2,000 annually and enjoy a minimum of six concerts together during the year, taking part in receptions before and after the musical performance. Circle members are also encouraged to meet the performers and have first-hand experience of encountering them on a personal and professional level . . . a treasured experience, as the Wigmore Hall attracts the finest musicians.

Members of the Circle have been delighted with the experiences of the past four years and particularly look forward to the annual party given in July. This event has proved to be a delightful meeting point for musicians and members and has formed and cemented many friendships.

The name given to this scheme was chosen as it seemed particularly appropriate given the fact that Arthur Rubinstein fell in love with the Hall when he made his debut in 1912. At his final public performance he requested that his audience 'keep coming back to this wonderful hall' and it is hoped that members of the Rubinstein Circle will continue to follow this advice! It is a tribute to his memory that so many have shown their loyal support and many more special events are planned for the future.

It is with great pride that I share the experience of being a member of such a loyal, supportive and caring group.

JACKIE ROSENFELD, *Trustee*

The Friends of Wigmore Hall

In a questionnaire detailing all aspects of the Friends of Wigmore Hall, members were asked how they viewed the Friends scheme and variously described their association as 'forming a network of like-minded people', providing 'financial support for a worthy institution; a sense of common interest', 'an expression of warmth towards the organisation' and 'a practical way of expressing thanks for the splendid music making at the Wigmore.'

The support and encouragement of the audience has always been integral to the life of the Hall, and this alliance led to the formation of the Friends when the Hall reopened after refurbishment in 1992. The founding Administrator was Magdalen Roberts who held the position until mid-1998.

Many Friends have actively supported the Hall by regular and frequent attendance over the years. Increasing their commitment by joining the membership scheme has provided the chance for them to become more closely involved with the Hall and its ventures, whilst also playing a practical role in building a solid financial foundation so vital for the Hall's continuing success.

The membership scheme provides a service for the Hall's loyal supporters by ensuring that members receive advance listings of all the events at the Hall and the chance to book ahead of the general public. Advance dates and details about artists are announced in *The Score* – the magazine for Friends – which also includes news of developments in the Hall and projects which are of interest to members. Friends are often keen to meet

Chamber Tots

fellow Friends and special events are arranged, which lend a sociable element to the advantages of membership. It is true to say that Friends can often find friends through their association with the Hall!

Over the years the contribution of Friends has actively supported festivals such as the Purcell Tercentenary celebrations (1993-4), the Britten Songs series (1994-5) and the Brahms Chamber Music Festival (1996). Many evenings have also been made possible by members lending their support, in recent years, to concerts given by artists such as Ian Bostridge, Felicity Lott, the Takács Quartet, Christine Schäfer and the Vienna Piano Trio, to name but a few.

Over and above their financial support of projects, Friends are often willing to help in other ways. Their views as audience members and frequent visitors to the Hall are sometimes canvassed and members have provided us with valuable advice on everything from the possible expansion of the Hall to the improvement of the catering facilities. The recent establishment of a committee of Friends has further emphasised the value and importance we place on the thoughts and views of our supporters.

A pool of practical support was sought from members in 1996 and a band of Volunteer Friends emerged, offering unselfish contributions of time and energy to the Hall's endeavours. Volunteers regularly join staff in the large-scale mailings which the Hall undertakes, thereby saving the Hall time and money. They also offer practical help with the restoration of the archives, assist with receptions and give visitors the benefit of their knowledge of the Hall when the building takes part in London Open House each year.

The passion and commitment of the people who support the Hall so wholeheartedly remain an inspiration for all who work here. We are fortunate to be able to share the wonderful music with an ever-growing body of such ardent Friends.

Nicolette Spera, *Friends Administrator*

The Publications

As Publications Manager at Wigmore Hall it is my responsibility to co-ordinate the publication of all the printed material that the Hall produces. This includes the preparation of the Master Series brochures, monthly diaries and posters, newspaper advertising and concert programmes – approximately 250 a year. A daunting task, and one that I couldn't possibly achieve without the assistance of my colleagues at the Hall, a small team of freelancers, and, in particular, our designer Peter Williamson, whose association with the Hall goes back some 20 years.

When I first started working with Peter 13 years ago all the brochures and programmes were still produced on typesetters – the material was co-ordinated at the Hall and then typed up by Peter's secretary. The development of computer design technology has dramatically changed the way in which they are now produced and has given Peter an opportunity to extend and develop his considerable design skills.

There are, however, many steps along the way before a brochure or programme is ready to send to Peter for the final production and printing. These involve various members of staff collating the material, a process which begins many months before the actual publication date.

Writing a few lines about each artist, gathering together quotes from the press – all of this is done by William Lyne's assistant Derek Archer, and then checked by William who will always add another quote or some additional information about the artist. Inevitably, there are delays in collating the material for a brochure or diary. Last minute changes of programme or cancellations can throw an already demanding schedule into disarray. Once the material has been gathered together I format the text and, in the case of Master Series brochures, make a rough layout, leaving space for pictures. This sounds simple but is, in fact, very time-consuming and difficult. I leave the final layout to Peter, who with his designer's eye can make a page look really good – to achieve this effect on one page can take hours. Numerous telephone conversations ensue regarding the placing of the text or a photo. Perhaps the text is too long and needs to be cut, should we use a different photo here, is it possible to get a colour photo of that artist?

The text and pictures are now in place and it is time to proof-read. Copies are given to other members of staff to check – this is very impor-tant as everyone finds something different. I read the alterations through to Peter who then makes the changes and sends me the corrected version. Once I am satisfied that the corrections have been made – although I usually find some more at this stage – the brochure is finally ready for Peter to prepare for the printer. A final colour proof will then arrive – unless we discover something seriously wrong changes are not made at this stage. After many weeks of hard work, the brochure is finally ready.

Producing the printed programmes presents a different set of prob-lems. Now that the brochure is printed, it is time to look through the programmes and consider the programme notes for each event. For the past couple of years I have worked with Lynne Walker, who commissions the notes for most of the events that appear in the Master Series brochure; programmes and leaflets that do not appear in this brochure are the responsibility of the artist or management that has hired the Hall for the evening. As we produce approximately 250 programmes a year, and sometimes six or seven a week, this has to be a very finely-tuned operation. Programme covers for the period are pre-printed, along with any advertising that is procured by the advertising agency and pages with the details of the Hall's various departments – Education, Friends and

Development. The information for the individual programme is collated about 10 days before the performance. Programme notes and biographies are now sent mostly via e-mail – how did we manage without it? The programmes are proof-read by my assistant, and are printed just a couple of days before the performance. We have learnt with experience that if the programmes are printed too far in advance there are invariably changes made to either the programme or the artist. By printing the programme at a late stage we can nearly always make the changes when necessary.

Finally, I would like to mention the Wigmore Hall archive. We are very fortunate to have an almost complete set of concert programmes, diaries and other artefacts dating from the inaugural concerts in 1901 up to the present day, with just a few gaps in the late 40s and 50s. The archive constitutes an irreplaceable record of the Hall's first hundred years and provides a unique insight into the history of the 20th century. We are currently undertaking the restoration of the 1901-1945 concert programmes, and we hope, in due course, to make the archive accessible to the public. Perhaps in a hundred years' time someone will be writing a book about the bicentenary of the Wigmore and looking at our current brochures, diaries and programmes with interest. How will they be produced one hundred years from now, I wonder?

PAULA BEST, *Publications Manager*

The Education Programme

§ *Beginnings.* The programme of education activities at the Wigmore Hall is a fairly recent development. In less than a decade at the end of its first century, Wigmore has developed and promoted a lively and vigorous range of activities which are designed to encourage active participation in chamber music.

It was in the summer months of 1982 that Sir Roy Shaw, as Secretary-General of the Arts Council, asserted the need for education in the arts as an indispensable accompaniment to support the arts. His definition of 'education' was broad, embracing not only 'that which happens to children in schools where the process begins', but the continuing 'life-long' discovery of oneself.

The substantial policy shift by the Arts Council in the mid-1980s had a profound influence upon arts organisations and artists. Those in receipt of public funds through the Arts Council, awakened to their responsibility to the wider community that supported their work and developed education activities as an arm of their artistic operation.

§ *The Wigmore focus.* The appointment of an Education Officer to the staff of the Wigmore Hall in 1994 followed a review of the possibilities and potential for developing an educational dimension to the already distinguished artistic enterprise. Funding such an initiative was never going to be easy, but with generous supporters, including Westminster City Council, a start was made under the leadership of Anne Willie. In a relatively short period of time and with modest resources, a series of pre-concert talks and in-depth lectures was launched, alongside a programme of school projects and teacher training sessions.

This was brought into sharp focus in 1996 when Ruth Goldstein took over as Education Officer, bringing with her the valuable experience she gained in a similar position with the London Symphony Orchestra's education department at the Barbican Centre. The heart of the Wigmore education programme continued to be firmly rooted in the high quality and international reputation of the artists and the Hall. Three distinctive features have sustained the development of the programme: the *range* of activities – from those for the very young to those in their retirement years; the *scope* of activities – from participation to appreciation; and the *balance* of activities – incorporating workshops, lectures and master classes. Notable additions to the programme during this time included folk fiddle workshops for violinists with classical experience, jazz events for all ages and abilities, and chamber tots, offering pre-school-aged children the opportunity to enjoy music at the Hall.

Collaborations with other organisations have led to the development of both the education programme and its participants. Successful partnerships with the Wallace Collection, Birkbeck College Faculty of Continuing Education and the Cavatina Chamber Music Trust continue to enrich the work of the department.

§ *The Education Programme*. A glance at the listings for the education programme shows the broad scope of its influence. Beverley Fell, appointed to succeed Ruth Goldstein in January 2000, has brought together a rich and varied programme which includes the Wigmore Study Group (for adults to discuss and engage with the chamber music repertoire), family and schools concerts supported by resources, and the development of outreach work through Chamber Tots in the Community. The work of the Education Manager is now assisted by a second member of staff, Rachel Selvidge, together with a small Advisory Committee which helps with the department's long-term planning.

Artists and composers have welcomed the new facet of Wigmore Hall, responding enthusiastically to promote and participate in the education programme. The artistry of Barbara Bonney and Graham Johnson provided a fitting celebration of the achievements of the education work of the Hall at a special concert at Spencer House in March 2000. Writing in the programme William Lyne gives his own testimony to the value of education: 'The music I heard in my youth certainly changed my life and I know of many others who have been similarly affected. The inspiration and development of young people is one of the main aims of our education department, together with the widening of the musical horizons of adult audiences.'

§ *The Future*. The Education Department of the Hall is now poised to develop a wider sphere of influence through the application of advanced technology. The high quality of its artistic programme and its international reputation places Wigmore at the very heart of the chamber music resource. In continuing to enrich and enhance people's lives the educational dimension is now firmly rooted.

JOHN STEPHENS, *Chairman, Education Advisory Committee*

PICTURE CREDITS

The Editor and The Wigmore Hall Trust wish to thank the following photographers and copyright holders for the use of their work: Cover photograph, frontispiece and full-colour half titles, Peter Aprahamian; title page art, Peter Williamson. 10 Zoë Dominic; 15 Carruthers; 17 Polygram; 20 Dünhöft, Köln; 22 Malcolm Crowthers; 27 Ingpen & Williams; 29 (top) Keith Saunders; 66 Decca/Vivianne Purdom; 69 EMI; 73 EMI Classics/Angus McBean; 81 Organisation Artistique International; 87 (top) Askonas Holt/Anthony Crickmay; 87 (bottom) Peter Schaff; 89 Richard Faulks/EMI Classics; 90 Decca/Suzie E. Maeder; 91 (top) Decca/Andrew Eccles; 91 (bottom) David Thompson/EMI Classics; 92 Hanya Chlala; 93 Vivianne; 95 Bill McKenzie; 96 Holger Badekow; 97 Clive Barda; 98 Jim Four; 101 Trevor Leighton; 102 David Tuck; 103 Hanya Chlala; 104 Malcolm Crowthers; 105 (top) Malcolm Crowthers; 105 (bottom) Gramophone/Bayley; 106 Ivan Pinkava; 107 Keith Saunders; 109 Ingpen & Williams; 111 Christian Steiner; 119 Gunnar Westergren; 120 (left) Tim Richmond; 137 EMI/David Farrell; 152 Aldeburgh Foundation; 163 (top) Philips/Alecio de Andrade; 163 (bottom) Suzie E. Maeder; 173 (bottom left) EMI; 173 (bottom right) Decca International; 188 (left) Frank Ockenfels. Every effort has been made to trace copyright holders; in the event of an error or omission please contact Wigmore Hall, 36 Wigmore Street, London W1U 2BP.